REAL MEN
ENJOY THEIR KIDS!

REAL MEN ENJOY THEIR KIDS!

HOW TO SPEND QUALITY TIME WITH THE CHILDREN IN YOUR LIFE

Wenda Goodhart Singer

Stephen Shechtman

Mark Singer

Illustrations by John R. Robinson

ABINGDON PRESS——————————— NASHVILLE

REAL MEN ENJOY THEIR KIDS!

Library of Congress Cataloging in Publication Data

SINGER, MARK, 1941–
  Real men enjoy their kids.
  1. Father and child. 2. Men—Family relationships.
  3. Child rearing. 4. Interpersonal relations.
  5. Social interaction. I. Singer, Wenda, 1944– .
  II. Shechtman, Stephen, 1951– . III. Title.
  HQ756.S545   1983   306.8′7   82-24317

ISBN 0-687-35598-2

MANUFACTURED BY THE PARTHENON PRESS AT
NASHVILLE, TENNESSEE, UNITED STATES OF AMERICA

For our children, David, Becky, and Seth,
who teach us about loving and learning

and

To our parents,
who helped us become the persons we are

CONTENTS

ACKNOWLEDGMENTS

To the many interested people who were important in our efforts to compile this book, we offer thanks. To Leah Evans for her excellent typing and editing skills which helped create our original manuscript. To Jo Anne Woody and the Virginia Commonwealth University staff who were instrumental in typing the final drafts. To Mildred Goodhart, Robert Goodhart, Gertrude Curtler, Kitty Cox, and Carol Uzzle for their suggestions and editorial comments. We appreciate the children who have shown us that men could be nurturant. A special thanks to Ellen Weiss, who helped Steve regain his sense of personhood and the strength to finish this manuscript. And finally, our thanks to Beatrice Saunders and Martin Bloom for their assistance and frequent boosts of morale.

AN OVERVIEW

YOU AND YOUR KIDS

Why don't you ever do anything with the kids? Has your wife ever said that to you? And have you ever felt guilty because you know you really don't spend as much time as you should with your kids?

There are probably endless reasons why you don't. You're too tired at the end of the day. Your mind is still on your job. There are countless chores to do around the house. It would cut into your time with your wife. And finding things to do with the kids would become just another chore to be attended to.

Let the pages of this book convince you that you are *very* important to those kids and that you can profit from time together as much as they can. Start with some of the activities that *you* think sound like fun. Have any necessary materials prepared. And concentrate on your child during the activity as attentively as you would concentrate on your boss. After a few tries, we predict that you'll be thinking of the "chore" as a pleasure.

All my niece and nephew want to do when they see me is "horse around." I don't know what else to do with them. My work with adults takes a lot of my time, and I don't really know kids. And I don't think they really know me.

In wanting to improve the quality of your relationship with your niece and nephew you have taken the first step. The horseplay you now enjoy is your "foot in the door," so to speak. You might find that some more organized physical activities are what you need. Several are suggested in Section Three under "Physical Dimension." Your constant exposure to adults obviously is not giving you any help with things kids would enjoy. Just skim through Section Two and check off some activities that appeal to you, and then consider whether your niece or nephew would be interested in any of them. The next time you are together, suggest a couple, and if they choose one, *have the materials available to carry it out.* The Comment portion of the activity will clue you in to its intended purpose. The better prepared you are, the more comfortable you will be in trying something new.

It's my turn to have the kids this weekend, but what am I going to do with them?

If you've ever had that thought and found yourself dreading the arrival of Friday evening, then this book is for you. It isn't necessary for you to be a "zoo daddy," providing special treat after special treat. There are some everyday kinds of things you can do that will result in quality time together. This book talks about ways to make simple routine activities meaningful and enjoyable. The Evaluation section at the end of each activity can help you decide whether you are using your weekends to build a stronger relationship with your children.

I just can't afford to give the kids the good time they always expect.

You already have a good relationship with your kids. What you are looking for now is a new stockpile of ideas—ideas that won't cost you an arm and a leg. The activities we outline in this book purposely do not require expensive materials. One starting point might be to complete the Adult's Interest Survey for yourself and the Child's Interest Survey for each of your children. Then look through the book for activities that match your interests.

What would my friends say if I told them I spent Saturday afternoon cutting out paper dolls with my daughter?

If you're worried about doing things with your kids that make you feel silly, remember that if you are not embarrassed about those things, your friends will probably accept them, too, just as they accept your chores around the house and your hobbies. When you flip through the pages of this book, you may find some activities that *you* would like. It could be fun to show off some piece of carpentry work that you and your daughter have made. But don't completely rule out the possibility of paper dolls (or knitting, or needlework—à la football player Rosie Greer). You would certainly learn to know your daughter better, and it might be fun to enter her imaginary world.

My girl friend and I would like to get married. Why can't I get her daughter to relate to me?

There are many reasons your friend's daughter may not be able or want to relate to you, but exploring those reasons is not the purpose of this book. The important thing is that you want to relate to her. In Section Two, we have provided evaluation questions for each activity we suggest, and by reading several, you may begin to see how you are *not* relating. That is a great first step. Then in Section Three, we deal with emotional and social, as well as other dimensions of development. You might find some hints there for helping the child realize that you really are interested in her as a person, not just because you love her mother. Further exploration of this book may give you some ideas about how to use some of your own skills and interests to promote better relations with this youngster.

We see the grandchildren just a couple of times a year. How can I get the best mileage from those visits?

You're probably also thinking about how it was to be a father and wondering how you'll rate as a grandfather. Do you have any special interest or hobby? Look over the "For Leisure Time" activities in Section Two, and they may give you some ideas about how to share your skills with your grandchildren. Do the children have hobbies or special talents of their own? Let them teach *you* something. Also, most children are curious about what their parents were like as youngsters. You can be their key to that knowledge. The Family History activity might be one way to proceed, or it might provide you with other ideas. Good luck in your visits together—may they be pleasant chapters in your continuing family history.

So, it is never too late to begin to build a relationship with the kids in your life, and this book will help you consider the many different ways this can be done. Your strongest asset is your desire and willingness to spend quality time with the children in your life.

MEN AND NURTURING

Until recently, a father's part in raising and nurturing children was given little attention. "Real men" tended to leave the kids to mom—men's job was to work to support the family and when they came home, to mete out the punishment that mom had decreed. Happily for fathers and their children, that attitude is changing. Society now acknowledges that real men do enjoy their kids. There is a growing emphasis on the importance of the bond between fathers and children. Men, as whole persons, realize that they provide a sense of security for their children in both emotional and material ways. They are central to the development of their children, who need their love and support. Men are realizing that they, as well as women, need to learn to be parents.

But fathers are not the only men in children's lives. Today

a household does not always include the child's biological mother or father. In this book we want to help any man, whether biological parent, or step-parent, or significant male figure in a child's life, to learn to be an effective model. Children develop best in an environment where love is expressed both verbally and nonverbally, and where they receive support as they continue to mature. More loving and meaningful relationships can grow between children and men as they share activities together. Here we provide ways for fathers, and for other adults, to build and to maintain positive relationships with children.

In *Real Men Enjoy Their Kids*, we focus on fathers and other male adults, emphasizing traditionally male activities. There are several reasons for this. First, most of the adults and role models that young children meet daily on a face-to-face basis are women. In addition to their mothers, most children's day-care workers, church school teachers, Cub Scout leaders, and elementary schoolteachers are women. What men do at work, at evening meetings, or when they are out bowling is often a mystery to children.

Boys need a father or some other significant man to serve as a model of male behavior. Girls who experience a warm and stable relationship with a mature male will find it easier to establish a mature relationship with a man when they are grown. It is true that TV, books, and other mass media have male "heroes," and a child who has no man to relate to can retreat to those media heroes for information on "proper" male behavior. But a genuine experience with a loving man can certainly help to counterbalance the sometimes questionable qualities of those idols.

Increasing attention is now being paid to the positive effect that bonding* has on a child's development and upon the quality of the relationship between parent and child. This bonding is strengthened as the adult and child spend time together. However, the important thing is not the *amount* of time, but the *kind* of time they share. *Undivided,*

Bonding is the emotional connection between parent and child.

unhurried, uncritical time together develops mutual affection and respect.

Finally, as fathers or other men participate in activities with their children, they are demonstrating the importance they place on their homes and families. There are many demands on adults, all requiring some time commitment, and by spending quality time (not merely a quantity of time) with their kids, fathers (and adults in general) show their children that the family is important.

Each of us must assess and reassess our priorities. We need to put our career in perspective with our family life. Men other than fathers who have some involvement with children also need to remember how important they are to those children and to consider the effect of a strong and loving relationship. Good relationships are far more important than material possessions. Children who are unhappy and maladjusted report that the greatest lack in their lives was not that of material comfort, but the lack of time and attention—in other words, the love—of their fathers or mothers.

Children have much to gain from meaningful relationships with men, despite the limitations that may exist—separation or divorce; lack of time, education, or money; the ability to be together only occasionally. With this book as a guide, each of us can learn to relate to our children and enjoy being with them.

LEARNING TO BE A FATHER

All fathers, whether we are forcefully aggressive or more reserved and gentle, have one thing in common: we all are learning how to parent. Few of us, however, examined our father role before we became one. The result is that we either rely heavily on skills we absorbed from our own parents, or we take a "seat of the pants" approach, learning while doing. And some of us do not attend to the parenting role at all. For you who are not fathers but do share close ties with a child, the task may seem even greater, for your main models would be grandfathers or uncles, who may have been either indulgent or austere.

Society's stereotyped thinking about parents works against fathers here. People tend to have limited expectations of men. A father traditionally is perceived as being a parent on a "sometime" basis, not really necessary to a child's growth and development. (A mother, on the other hand, is viewed as the one person essential to child-rearing.) This bias not only establishes a low set of expectations for men, but tends to stifle our creativity in becoming warm, sensitive, and imaginative with our children. Recently, this situation may have altered slightly, with the rise in male-headed households and with more emphasis being put on such practices as having husbands present in the delivery room. It is no longer as easy or acceptable for those of us who are still the primary breadwinners in our households to use that as an excuse for not spending quality time with our children. New types of family groups, the presence of men in elementary classrooms, and such programs as Big Brothers are slowly drawing attention to the importance in children's lives of men who are other than fathers.

Nonetheless, there is still a need for men to develop an awareness of our own parent/nurturing potential, based both on our interests apart from the parent role (or leader role) and on our role in the home.

A number of steps are suggested below which can be used to gain such an awareness and a realization of the creative potential possible in parent/child relationships.

1. First, assess the degree and quality of closeness you now have with your children and evaluate whether these are satisfactory to you and to your children.

2. Survey your own personal and professional interests and decide how you can best integrate these with activities

that coincide with the growth and development of your children.

3. Examine the time you now spend with your children and review the type and quality of your activities.

4. Start involving your children in your own personal and professional interests from time to time. For example, if you spend a great deal of time at your place of work, decide how to take your children with you when you work extra hours. This obviously will depend to a large degree on the age of your children. Depending on your job responsibilities, allow your children to spend time doing parallel or similar activities while you work. Older children may actually be able to assist you. We know one parent whose child helped by correcting the objective portions of the test papers he was grading. Another father, a carpenter, took his child along to help him complete a job.

5. Purposely set aside certain times during the day especially for your child. Building in time on a regular basis will help you establish a routine, and may also help you think of different activities to carry out at other times.

6. Spontaneous activities which result from the daily routine of family life are natural ways to begin having "together time." Going to the store or raking the leaves are just two of numerous "things to do." We hope the ideas in this book will help you think of others.

7. Don't be overly concerned about the amount of time you can spend with your child. Some quality time is better than none, and children are capable of understanding that you are doing the best you can. Remember that it is better to spend some real sharing time with your child than to regret the fact that you are not spending any.

8. Don't be overly critical of your performance. Parenting, or any close relationship with a youngster requires that you observe your interaction as a process—not as a sporting event, winning and losing. You are trying to make connections with your child, not tutor a genius.

9. Keep in mind that your child needs room to fail. You owe it to your child not to diminish his or her self-concept

because he can't catch your NFL-style football passes or she can't recite the Gettysburg Address. Einstein failed math. The world is a judgmental place, so home should be a supportive environment. Any necessary criticism should be as constructive as possible. For example, if your child is holding a saw incorrectly, you can say that you would like to show a safer and easier way—but only after you have praised the first effort.

10. Think of your own father's style of interaction. What were his positive teachings? What negatives should you discard? Parents and other adult models teach both positives and negatives. The trick is to teach your child to self-select the best qualities—that is, high moral values, sharing.

YOUR CHILD

In learning to relate well to your children, you may find it helpful to look at their development in total perspective. This total-developmental approach includes several dimensions: the social, the emotional, the cognitive, the physical, and the spiritual development of a person.

The *social* dimension centers on how well we relate to others. What type of relation does your child have with family members? Does he have friends? If so, are there many, or just one or two close friends? What type of role does your child play in these relationships—is she a follower, or a leader?

As you look at the *emotional* aspects of development, be sure to include the full range of emotions. Be aware of the types of emotion displayed, their degree of intensity, and whether they are appropriate to the situation. Is your child highstrung? Does he explode at the slightest provocation? or does he have a long-burning fuse? Does she never cry? or does she cry without cause? It probably is important to remember, also, that certain types of emotion may be caused by either frustrating or successful experiences. Your children should be allowed to have emotions, as well as to evaluate and channel them.

Cognitive development includes what traditionally have been thought of as academic interests: reading and math readiness, ability to understand directions, and abstract thinking. In terms of this book, cognitive development also includes *how* your child is learning. Is he afraid to make a mistake? Is she fearful of you as a man? On the other hand, you can ask yourself, "What do I really know? Can I teach? Will the child learn from me?"

The *physical* dimension includes health, physical and athletic skills, body changes, and a sense of body awareness. You might look first at the extent of your child's physical development. Then look at yourself. How aware of your own body are you? How freely do you move? Do you enjoy sports?

During childhood, much growth and bodily change takes place. Children progress from reflex hand movements to holding large objects, to manipulating pencil and scissors. As their muscles strengthen they become less clumsy. Some children have a natural athletic ability, while others are more sedentary. For many, adolescence begins during childhood, and their bodies mature even before they become teenagers.

As you consider physical development, some general questions are appropriate. Is your child more, or less clumsy than others his age? Is he a healthy weight? Is there opportunity for physical exercise each day? What is your child's size in relation to others the same age? Is your child comfortable with her body? Does she understand how it functions?

Spiritual development includes a focus on the inner life, God, creation, a consciousness of the spirituality of all creatures, and the preservation of life from an ecological perspective. It includes such higher moral teachings as sharing, loving oneself and others, respect for others, and the sanctity of life. The spiritual dimension extends beyond any weekly religious observances, although these are certainly not to be discounted. You need to be aware of your own references to these issues and the increasing clarity with which your children understand and can express spiritual/religious concepts. For example, a small child may imagine God as a Large Man in the sky, but an older child has the ability to expand this concept to think of a Spirit whose love always surrounds us. As a child matures, there is an increased feeling of respect for this earth and of responsibility for the care of the plants, animals, and people on it.

As an adult using a total-developmental approach, you are trying to see your child in a comprehensive fashion. Your aim is to gain a broad view of your child's ability, rather than focus on one or two dimensions. For example, your goal would be to see your child as a good athlete but a poor reader, as shy around adults but at ease around other children. This approach helps you accept your child for who he or she is: a person with both strengths and weaknesses.

In the following paragraphs we describe some general characteristics of children at two broad stages of development. Remember, though, that each person is an individual and progresses at his or her individual rate. Your child is unique and should not be labeled as being entirely in one stage or another. In attempting to offer some general guidelines on development, we have grouped characteristics into those most common to each stage.

YOUNGER CHILD (0–6 YEARS)

The younger child wants very much to please adults. The peer group is not nearly as important as the parent figures. During these years both boys and girls need a meaningful relationship with a male figure. Infants and toddlers see their mothers, and sometimes other females, as the primary figures in their lives, partly because these are the persons who usually supply their biological needs. Fathers and other men who are frequently around a child become more important as a child matures and learns to take an interest in the world at large. From the man in the family, boys learn behaviors appropriate for males and girls learn how to relate to men.

Young children learn best from concrete experiences rather than from abstractions. For example, a lesson on "the changing seasons" is much more effective during a walk in the woods in the fall than in the living room on the Fourth of July. Since your child is focusing on your behavior (you are an important model), you will notice that he or she is listening to you, imitating you, and learning from you.

But your role is also to be a good listener. Each of us desires positive feedback that we are being effective, but don't rely simply on your child's ability to verbalize questions and responses, since this may not be well developed. *Young children will exhibit much nonverbal reaction.* And they will often show what they have learned after the learning event is over. Does your child talk about the walk by the ocean? or use the experience in make-believe play?

A younger child will remember the more observable characteristics of an experience. For example, if you watched a cowboy show in which the good guy defeated the bad guy, the child might say the cowboy shot a gun, had a fight, and put the bad guy in jail. The older child might report that the bad guy broke the law, the good guy helped the pretty girl because he wanted to marry her, and this was an example of good defeating evil.

On the other hand, the younger generation as a whole is brighter, in terms of world awareness and knowledge, than we were. Don't be frightened by this precociousness. You have much to offer—yourself.

OLDER CHILD (7–12 YEARS)

In spending time with older children, your rewards are perhaps more concrete and immediate. *They can understand the world in a more adult manner, are verbally competent, and are desirous of relating to and pleasing you.* At the same time, the older they are, the more sophisticated they are in their ability to reject you.

On the developmental side, *an older child can think about both concrete and abstract ideas.* For example, in planning a trip to the moon, an older child could ponder a list of important items to include on the packing list (perhaps chocolate bars versus air tanks).

During these years, the peer group rises in importance. This means that sometimes your parent role will conflict with the peer group's values or behavior. The concept of the family, especially of identifying oneself as a member of that family, develops over time. The ideal situation is that a loving and mutually respecting set of interactions has already been developed by the time your children reach their teen years. If that is indeed the case with you, remember that the relationship between father and child needs to be continually nurtured; the relationship becomes more critical when you come into conflict with the values of the peer group when trying to teach morality and values.

On the other hand, your relationship may not be anywhere near ideal. It may be clouded by years of inadequate attention or communication problems. But you can improve that relationship through your conscious effort and your awareness of the importance of the male role. This may require the ability to forgive and forget; you may need to risk rejection by saying, "I'm sorry we haven't been communicating, spending time together." It is sometimes difficult to forgive oneself for being less than adequate, but by becoming aware and trying to improve the relationship, it is often possible to reverse the situation. In a world that tends to teach the older child to be independent very quickly, remember that your children need your support and guidance if they are to develop their greatest potential.

HOW TO USE THIS BOOK

Real Men Enjoy Their Kids is not a kind of cookbook, which will mechanically result in a magical transformation of the relationship between you and your child. Its purpose is rather to help you begin to enjoy your child by suggesting things you can do together. As you work and play, you will be exploring your child's uniqueness. The time factor, your genuine willingness to take time with your child, is probably the most important ingredient in your successful use of the activities. This point cannot be overemphasized.

You will find that almost anything done with a child takes more time than if done alone. This is especially true if being together opens up informal conversation. The by-product of *talking* with your child may be one of the greatest advantages of engaging in these activities. So don't get involved in a complicated project if your time is severely limited. A "junk collage" is meaningless if it is produced in a rushed manner, the only object being to complete it in the shortest possible time. If your six-year-old can say, "Let's talk, Dad," and expect a positive response, count yourself fortunate. You may be avoiding some major communication problems during the turbulent teenage years.

You will notice that a number of the activities, especially those for older children, are staged in several periods of time, perhaps extending over a week or longer. Thus there is built-in follow-through to establish continuity in your relationship and also to provide a focus of common interest in everyday conversation.

If you have more than one child, you may find it better, at least at first, *to do an activity with one child at a time.* For one thing, it probably would be easier to orchestrate. Also, the time together is more special if it is a private one-on-one situation. We do not want to imply that these ideas should never be carried out by the whole family together. Building rapport among several family members is also a worthy goal. But now you may ask, How do I actually carry out the ideas in the book?

★ The first step is to complete the Interest Sheets—one for you and one for each child. They are found in the back of the book. The information on the sheets can serve as your starting point in selecting specific activities and convenient times for you and for each child. Don't be surprised if you discover new interests as you go along.

★ The activities are separated into broad categories—household chores, leisure-time activities, world-of-work activities, family-time activities—to help you select a variety of projects. It is also a way to identify your roles and interests and those of your children and allows you to become accustomed to doing different kinds of activities.

★ Each project is divided into two sections, one for younger children and one for older. The step-by-step directions for each age group are preceded by a list of materials needed to carry out the project. The directions are followed by a paragraph or two of comment on the general usefulness of this kind of sharing time. Finally, an evaluation section suggests ideas to consider as you carry out the activity.

★ You may find it helpful to skim through the activity ideas and mark those that, at first glance, appeal to you.

★ Look through the "Men and Nurturing" chapter of Section One and try to determine, at least in an initial sense, who you are as a man and as a father, and the kind of relationship you would like with your child.

★ Think about some of the characteristics of your child. The "Your Child" chapter in Section One should help with this.

★ Look over the activities again and mark those you think your child might enjoy and be able to handle. Don't immediately categorize your child as "younger or "older." The headings are general guides. Interests and particular abilities are more important than the labels in this book.

★ Preplanning is important. Select a couple of ideas you would enjoy and that you think your child would enjoy.

Sometimes you can suggest activities spontaneously; at other times it is better to plan ahead. A choice of activities should be offered at least occasionally. And be aware that children have ideas of their own. Ask your child for suggestions.

Part of preplanning is understanding the directions. It is aggravating for a child to be fidgeting while you try to figure out the next step. Besides, concentrating on the book precludes giving attention to your child. And it is your child and the relationship that are important. An activity is only a means to that end.

Another step in preplanning is to gather the materials that will be needed. Perhaps you have participated in a project which required so much time to get ready that much of its appeal was lost. We have attempted to use materials that are commonly found around the house or that can be obtained free or inexpensively. There is nothing wrong with having an older child take partial responsibility for collecting any needed items for a future project. Younger children might find it difficult to wait.

★ The Comment section at the end of each activity suggests the achievement of a specific relationship or skill. It focuses on the value of the particular project. It can help you become more aware of your increasing skill in carrying out special times with your children.

★ The Evaluation section gives specific ideas to think about as you assess that particular activity and your time with your child. It is not meant to point out success or failure, but to assist in promoting continued growth.

★ You may choose to use the three Processing Sheets found in the Appendix of this book. They are designed to be used after you have completed 12 to 16, 24 to 32, and 33 to 45 activities. These sheets serve as a follow-up to the Interest Sheets filled in before engaging in the activity and are meant to help you reflect on the growth that is taking place. You can indicate there: (1) discoveries you are making about yourself and your child; (2) ways the activities are or are not helping to maintain or improve your relationship; and (3) areas needing continued improvement.

★ The third section of this book highlights each area of human development. Use these as your interest warrants. The material can be useful in helping you make sure you are giving attention to each dimension of development.

SUMMARY

In *Real Men Enjoy Their Kids,* we ask you to consider your importance to the children in your life and to understand yourself, them, and your potential as an effective role model. We want to help you become aware of your children from a comprehensive point of view, taking into account the social, emotional, cognitive, physical, and spiritual development of each child. The activities we have selected relate to all these areas and also suggest enjoyable ways to spend time together. Underlying the whole book is our belief that men have a significant role to play in providing love and support for their growing children.

This handbook cannot be all things to all men. It is not meant to be all-inclusive. The activities it suggests are just that—suggestions. But the book can help each of you find ways to spend quality time with the children in your life, because "real men enjoy their kids."

ACTIVITIES

HOUSEHOLD CHORES

THE CAR

Younger Child—Car-Care Kit

Materials: large sectioned box, such as an egg-carton or bottled-juice box; magic markers *or* construction paper, scissors, glue

1. Ask for an empty box at the grocery.
2. Parent should cut off the lid.
3. Decorate with magic markers, if your child has permission to use them (the ink *will* stain clothing)—*or*—cut shapes from construction paper and glue them to the outside of the box.
4. Store car-washing materials in one half of the box and car-waxing materials in the other half.
5. Glue a sheet of paper to one end to record supplies that need to be replenished.
6. During cooler weather, store the kit in a trash bag.

Comment

Many fathers have undoubtedly enjoyed having younger children wash hubcaps, hose down the car (and be hosed themselves), and/or rub the dried wax with a soft cloth until the car shines. The car-care kit extends the enjoyment by providing a way to prepare for car washing.

Evaluation
1. Did you and your child have fun?
2. Was there general conversation while you decorated the box?

Older Child—Driving Readiness

Materials: large cardboard box; stool, chair, or wooden box; masking tape; knife or large scissors; newspaper

1. Ask for a large cardboard box at the grocery.
2. Measure an automobile steering wheel (it may be necessary to do this prior to beginning the activity).
3. Draw the shape of the steering wheel on one side of the box.
4. Cut out "wheel."
5. Cut 2 rectangles about the length and width of your child's shoe from another side of the box.
6. Crumple a double sheet of newspaper and tape it firmly to the back of one rectangle.

7. Repeat step 6 with the other rectangle.
8. Have your child sit on the stool or wooden box.
9. Tape the rectangles with the taped-on newspaper to the floor in front of your child, within easy reach of the feet, while child holds "wheel" in hands.
10. Demonstrate how to turn the wheel for right and left turns and how to press the gas pedal to move faster and the brake to slow down.
11. Play a game of giving directions and watching for the correct response. A correct response should get a nod and a smile; an incorrect response an imitation of an auto horn and a smile. The object is first, to have fun, and second, to begin to learn some rudiments of driving.
12. Exchange places, allowing your child to give you directions.

Comment

From an early age, children are eager to be old enough to drive. The Soap-box Derby is a reflection of this natural interest. This activity makes use of some simple objects and imagination to help you teach your child some of the rudiments of driving. Note—you could vary this game with an imaginary car and practice with "pretend" steering wheel, turn signals, brake, and gas pedal.

Evaluation

1. Were you able to pretend without feeling silly?
2. Was your child comfortable, or uncomfortable, about giving you directions?

GRASS

Younger Child—Grass House

Materials: adult rake; grass cuttings; child's rake (optional); trash bag (optional)

1. Take turns raking grass into piles. Experiment with both sides of the rake.

2. Carry small piles to one big pile (or fill the trash bag).
3. Place heaped-up rows of grass to make imaginary walls for a house.
4. Take turns "designing" new rooms. You can talk about how grass feels, how it clings, how it stains.
5. If child is old enough, play game of instructing each other to go from one room to another.
6. When child begins to tire, place grass cuttings into bags for disposal.

Comment

Many children are at their parents' heels when grass is being mowed. This activity provides a surprise when you have completed it. Do not promise an activity if you plan to mow the entire yard and will be exhausted when you finish, *or* if there would not be enough time for leisurely "home construction."

Evaluation

1. Were you able to take part in the activity without becoming "fidgety"?
2. Was the child able to imagine the house and the various rooms?

Older Child—Seed Experiment

Materials: 3 or 4 samples of grass seed; fertilizer, if recommended; 2 trowels (or hoes and rakes); several sticks; string or twine; yardstick; watering can or hose

1. Choose a bare portion of your yard in which to stake out 3 or 4 squares (depending on the number of seed samples).
2. Lay the yardstick on the ground and push a 6" to 8" stick in the ground at each end of the yardstick.
3. Do the same for the remaining three sides. (You may need to change the position of the sticks to approximate a square shape.)
4. With the trowels, dig up the soil inside the square deep enough to loosen it (2 to 3"). If you prefer, and the child is allowed to use the tool, a hoe may be used.
5. With the sides of the trowel, or with the hoe, break the soil into small pieces.
6. Sprinkle one sample of grass seed into the square.
7. With hands or rake, mix the seeds with the soil.
8. Pat the soil down over the seeds.
9. Add fertilizer, if needed.
10. Water the soil lightly.
11. Wind string or twine around the sticks to "fence in" the square.
12. Repeat the procedure for the other squares. (This can be done on subsequent days.)
13. Repeat the watering twice a week or when the soil becomes dry.
14. Each week, ask your child for a progress report on each sample of grass seed.

15. Allow your child to decide which type of seed is most appropriate and allow him or her to make the actual purchase of the correct quantity for the remaining bare spots.

Comment

There always seems to be a place in every lawn on which grass has not grown well. This activity allows your child to be of particular assistance in deciding which seed will grow best on that spot. Depending on the attention span of the child, this activity could be divided into more than one activity period. The best time for this activity is the spring or early fall. Do not begin this activity unless you intend to reseed a bare portion of your lawn. Respect grows as your child observes your follow-through on his or her efforts.

Evaluation

1. Was your child able to use the tools appropriately?
2. How well were you able to work together?

CLEANING UP I

Younger Child—Cleaning the Garage, Basement, Attic

Materials: broom; dustpan; boxes or trash bags or cans

1. Introduce the idea that all adults have cleaning-up tasks to do.
2. Ask, "What will we need if we are going to get rid of all that trash in the garage (attic, shed)?"
3. Gather the materials your child names, or if you have already gathered them, say, "Well, it seems you know what we need. Can you help me carry these things? Let's get to work."
4. Separate trash from salvageables.
5. While separating, you can count boxes, pretend you are a steam shovel, tell your child what a good helper he or she is.
6. Place the trash in cans, bags, or boxes.
7. Sweep the area clean.

8. When your child tires, use the broom and have him or her hold the dustpan.

Comments

Children need to learn that home chores are important for maintenance. It is important to show your child how he or she can help. Remember, your child may tire and should be allowed to stop. Perhaps you could clean up part of the area one day and part on another day.

Evaluation
1. Was this activity successful?
2. Did you and your child enjoy your time together?

Older Child—Laundry Day

Materials: paper and pencils; large sheet of paper; clothes baskets or hampers; clothespins if needed

1. Introduce the concept that each family member is connected to the others in the household. Each member can be responsible for maintaining specific tasks.
2. Gather family members together. Give each one a pencil and paper. Direct them to list as many as they can of the tasks required to maintain the operation of the household. Ask each person to list at least three. (Those who cannot write can dictate their lists to other members of the family.)
3. List all the tasks on a large sheet of paper. Write the names of the person(s) responsible for it beside each task. Hang the sheet on the wall.
4. Compare the types and number of responsibilities. Point out that some tasks take more time than others, or that some are shared by a number of people.
5. Then tell your child that you and he or she will do the laundry next time.
6. When laundry needs to be done, let your child gather the clothing.

7. Separate some of the clothing into piles by color and fabric. Ask your child to finish the separating.
8. Load the washer.
9. Ask your child to read the soap box and measure out the detergent and any other additives desired.
10. Share the responsibility of transferring clothes to the dryer or clothesline.
11. Point out how well your child is helping.
12. Take the clothes from the dryer or line and fold or hang on hangers. Discuss which (fold or hang) should be done with each piece.
13. Allow your child to express his or her reaction to the task. When you finish, write down the amount of time it took to complete the task.

Comment

It is advisable to help a child learn daily living tasks. These responsibilities are best learned in a gradual and nonpunitive way. The goal is for your child to eventually bear full responsibility for a task.

Evaluation

1. Did your child express many positive and negative feelings?
2. List his or her verbal statements.
3. What did you say in response? Are you satisfied with your responses?

CLEANING UP II

Younger Child—Trash and Treasures

Materials: 4 large grocery sacks; magazine; scissors; crayon

1. Open four large grocery sacks and fold down the tops so they will stay open.
2. In the magazine, ask your child to find pictures of: (1) a glass bottle, (2) a metal can, and (3) a newspaper. Cut out the pictures and paste one on each of the three sacks. On the fourth sack, draw a big "?".

3. At a designated time each day, walk around inside or outside the house with your child, looking for empty bottles, cans, or newspapers. (Note: returnable bottles should be stored in their cartons). Also look for "treasures" that might be fun to use at a later time (like foil, gum wrappers, bottle caps, egg cartons, cereal boxes, plastic bottles, etc.). These are placed in the "?" sack. The other items are placed in the appropriate sacks. The person who empties bottles and cans will need to cooperate by rinsing them thoroughly when emptied and checking to be sure the cans have no sharp edges.

4. Call your sanitation department to see if they collect separated items at special times or places. If not, a salvage business may take several weeks' supply of cans. Scouts and church groups usually have paper

drives. At collection time, let your child help set the papers out, or go with you to the collection point. Even if cans and bottles are not collected separately, they will be separated from the rest of the trash and thus save garbage can space.

5. At the end of each week, or every two weeks, empty out the "?" bag. Talk together about what you might be able to do or make with your treasures. Your child may have some excellent ideas. Plastic bottles for water play or tub time, a collage glued on cardboard or construction paper, a game using pebbles tossed into sections of an egg carton, buildings or vehicles made from boxes printed or otherwise decorated—these are just a few idea starters.

6. Use the "?" trash to make a treasure.

7. Throw away all unused articles and start collecting again.

Comment

Looking for trash at a certain time each day will assure you of some sharing time and may help to build a habit of cleaning up. It places a value on at least a modicum of neatness and gives your child a feeling of sharing a responsibility with his or her father. It should make it easier to give each of you an additional picking-up responsibility later on. Your child might assume the duty of putting all the dirty clothes in the hamper. You might give yourself the same job, if needed, or some other job, such as emptying wastepaper baskets.

Separating trash introduces the idea of conservation and the "?" bag can encourage children to use their imaginations to make use of materials at hand, rather than relying entirely on store-bought entertainment.

Evaluation

1. How well did you and your child use your imaginations in thinking of a use for the items in the "?" bag?

2. Does your child seem to have some concept of conservation?

Older Child—Cleaning Up Exchange

Materials: paper; pencil

1. Let your child identify a cleaning-up chore that you tend to neglect; then identify a chore of your child's that he or she neglects. You both should choose *either* a weekly or a daily chore.
2. Each of you now determines two possible things you could do to reward the other for performing that chore. The other person can decide which reward to choose. (This might involve a little bartering.) Decide how many times each can forget and still be rewarded.
3. List your names on a sheet of paper and draw a chart with spaces for six weeks (or six days—whichever period of time you have selected). Place an X in a space for each time the chore is completed.
4. At the end of the time period, share the rewards earned.
5. Repeat the procedure until the chore is done automatically or until either party decides to stop.

Comment

An obvious result of this exercise can be a neater home (or yard or car). Just as significant will be the experience of planning together, thinking of each other's likes and dislikes, and sharing something of yourselves. Mutual respect grows in an atmosphere where a parent is willing to learn new behaviors as well as expecting improvement from a child.

Evaluation

1. Do you feel you showed respect for your child? Did your child show respect for you?
2. Was your child able to identify, without feeling embarrassed, a chore that you neglect?
3. Were both of you able to continue the activity for the specified time period?

CLEANING UP III

Younger Child—Wastebaskets

Materials: full wastebaskets; trash bags or can

1. Say to your child, "We have a job to do today. We need to empty the wastebaskets."
2. Allow your child to carry the trash bags and help you empty the baskets.
3. Count the baskets. How many are in the bathrooms? bedrooms? laundry room?
4. Count the number of trash bags filled.
5. Allow your child to help dispose of the bags.

Comment

Your child can learn to place trash in the wastebaskets as well as empty them. Trash collection is a regular task that is necessary for home maintenance. As a follow-up, you might have your child empty the small wastepaper baskets him- or herself. Be sure to praise that effort.

Evaluation

1. Did you enjoy this task?
2. What attitudes is your child learning?
3. Did your child see the activity as fun, or as a chore?

Older Child—Trash Collection

Materials: full wastebaskets; trash bags/cans

1. As a follow-up to the listing of home-maintenance tasks (see Cleaning Up I—Older Child) ask your child to gather the trash.
2. In the case of two or more children, ask them to take turns dumping baskets, holding trash bags, tying bags. You may need to assign the various tasks to avoid squabbles; next time, reverse the tasks. Also try letting your children assign the tasks.
3. Direct your child to assign you a role in the task. Allow him or her to attempt to solve any problems.

4. Deliver the trash bags to the place of pickup.
5. Go back to the job sheet. List both your child's name and your name and note the amount of time consumed. Compare it with the time spent on other tasks completed by other family members.
6. As a follow-up, guide a discussion with all the family members on family-living tasks. Allow your child to be responsible for some of the other tasks.

Comment

A major goal is to allow your child to experience daily-living tasks with the opportunity to switch to another job. He or she will gain experience from guiding you in gathering the trash. In this way, your child can learn to lead and to complete a task.

Evaluation

1. Were you able to allow your child to direct you?
2. What attitude does the child seem to be developing toward home-maintenance tasks?

GARDENING

Younger Child—Pretend Garden

Materials: seed catalogue; large piece of paper (brown wrapping paper is best); string; scissors; cellophane tape; masking tape

1. Sit with your child and take turns naming vegetables and fruits in the seed catalogue. This is a nonthreatening way to learn the names of unfamiliar foods.
2. When your child offers a positive opinion about some food, put a * beside its picture.
3. Repeat steps 1 and 2 at more than one sitting, if your child seems to be enjoying the activity.
4. At a later time, make a pretend garden plot. First, place the paper on the floor. Tell your child that you both will "plant" his or her favorite foods in the "garden."

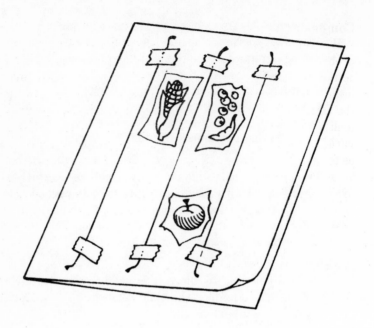

5. Use string to divide the rows of the garden, extending pieces from one side of the paper to the other. One of you can hold the string while the other cuts it.
6. Tape the string to both edges of the paper. Make 3 or 4 garden rows.
7. Cut your child's favorite foods from the catalogue.
8. Tape the pictures in the rows on the paper.
9. Leave the garden on the floor in an out-of-the-way place *or* tape it to the wall with masking tape. (Other kinds of tape will mar the wall.)
10. Put scissors, string, and tape away.
11. Later, tell your child that you are pretending you don't remember what you did and ask him or her to tell you about it. Identify the procedure and the favorite foods.
12. This activity can be repeated, using pictures of flowers.

Comment

Whether or not you order seeds from a catalog, you probably have enjoyed thumbing through the pages. This activity allows your child to imitate you with his own interests in mind and to express likes and dislikes. During the activity, you will also have the opportunity to reinforce feelings about the wonder of the growth process and the variety of foods, trees, and flowers that are in the world for us to enjoy and care for. If you do not have a seed catalog, get an address from your local lawn-and-garden store and send for one, or use an order blank from a magazine.

Evaluation

1. Did your child ask to repeat the activity?
2. Did each of you tell the other about your favorite foods?
3. Were there smiles and laughter when you pretended you did not know what project you had just completed and your child explained it to you?
4. Was your child able to manipulate the scissors and tape?

Older Child—What Makes a Garden Grow?

Materials: 12 vegetable seedlings; 3 peanut-butter or jelly jars; trash bag; 2 or 3 sticks; bucket; trowel; watering can or hose; small outdoor plot *or* flower box

1. Purchase 12 very young vegetable plants. (These are the cheapest. Or you could use some you have started from seed.)
2. Divide seedlings into 4 groups. You can plant one group while your child watches. Your child can plant the other groups while you watch. One group should be planted in the bucket.
3. Cover one group of plants with peanut-butter or jelly

jars, pushed into the soil. Water twice a week if there is no rain, but do not loosen soil around them.

4. Cover one group of plants with a dark trash bag. Sticks can be pounded into the ground, with the bag draped over them tent-fashion. The bag can be split down the sides so the ends can be folded over to prevent light from reaching the plants, but it should be loose enough that air can reach them. Water twice a week if there is no rain, and loosen soil with a trowel.

5. Do not water the group of plants in the bucket. Keep them outside to get air and sunlight. Bring the bucket inside to a sunny window if there is any chance of rain. Loosen the soil around the plants twice each week.

6. Water the fourth group of plants weekly if there is no rain, and loosen the soil around them.

7. Each week, examine the four groups of plants *with* your child to determine the effect of light, air, and water on their growth.

8. Pick, clean, and eat any vegetables at harvest time. Thank each other for the work involved in growing the food. If it is your custom, offer thanks to God for seeds that grow into food.

Comment

School science classes repeatedly emphasize the principle that plants need air, water, and sunlight in order to grow. Throughout the growth cycle of your garden, discuss the effect of these elements. Remember, sunlight not only assists in plant growth but can also parch soil and burn leaves. Air in the form of wind can destroy or injure plants. Too much water causes roots to rot and too little causes them to wither, and so on. Ask your child what he or she thinks the current weather (at any given time) will do to the garden. It builds a child's self-esteem to be included in adult conversation. Older children's science experiments in school, and possibly their 4-H involvement, expose them to the world of growing things. If you garden, this activity will give you the opportunity to share one of your interests with your child and also will reinforce the information learned at school.

You may want to help your child start seeds indoors in flats. Older children who express an interest might be given responsibility for a particular vegetable in the family garden, from planting to eating time.

A pocket of annual flower seeds could replace the vegetable seedlings. And for those without garden space, a flower box could be substituted for actual space outdoors.

Evaluation

1. Did your child understand why the plants reacted as they did? Did he or she ask questions?
2. Were you able to allow your child to plant the three groups of seedlings without taking over or giving unasked-for advice?
3. Was there a sense of wonder concerning the growth process?

BUDGETING

Younger Child—Budgeting for Leisure

Materials: paper; pen; magazine; construction paper *or* play money; masking tape; scissors

1. Think of 5 of your child's favorite family activities. On separate sheets of paper, either draw or glue pictures from a magazine to represent each activity. On the upper right hand corner of each sheet, write the number corresponding to the approximate number of dollars it costs the family to engage in that activity.
2. Cut rectangles from construction paper or any heavy paper in the approximate size and shape of actual paper money. Mark $1 in the center of each bill. Make enough "money" to purchase three or four activities. (Use only the $1 bills if using play money.)
3. Tape the activity sheets to the wall (at your child's eye level) or lay them side by side on the floor.

4. Give your child the bills. Explain that the numbers on the sheets correspond to the number of bills it takes to participate in the activity.
5. Allow your child to "buy" as many activities as he or she has bills. As each activity is purchased, that sheet is given to your child.
6. Reverse roles and purchase activities from your child.
7. The second or third time this game is played, you can begin to discuss why each activity has its particular value. Let your child tell you the various costs involved: gas, price of admission, snacks, picnic food, and so on.

Comment

Children can begin to learn the cost of activities and objects at an early age. The use of favorite activities is an attention-getter. This game can be referred to when budgeting questions arise in the course of family living.

Evaluation

1. Did your child see the relationship between the activity and its cost in "money"?
2. Was your child interested, or do you think he or she was engaging in the activity just to please you?

Older Child—Meal Planning

Materials: pen or pencil; large sheet of paper; masking tape; construction paper and scissors *or* play money; notebook paper

1. Make a chart listing the prices of foods that are commonly eaten in your home. The price should be the cost of serving that item to the whole family at one meal. (Use weekly store ads found in the newspaper or note and jot down the prices after returning from shopping trips.) The chart can be typed, printed, or written on a large sheet of paper and taped to the wall.
2. Cut rectangles from construction paper or any heavy paper in the approximate size and shape of actual

paper money. Mark $1 in the center of each bill. Make enough "money" to equal the approximate amount spent by your family for food during Saturday and Sunday (the days *not* influenced by lunches at school and work). (Use only the $1 bills if using play money.)

3. Prepare another chart on notebook paper as illustrated below. Have extra paper handy in case new charts are needed. Note: you know your child best. Prepare a chart for only one day, if you think planning for two days would cause frustration.

Day	Meal	Dish	Food Items

4. Give your child the bills and ask him or her to use that "money" to buy food for an imaginary weekend, choosing items from your prepared list and inserting them on the notebook-paper chart. Allow for several changes of mind; here you may need the extra charts.
5. Depending on your child's attention span, talk about the things that taste good together; which is the most expensive and which the least expensive meal. No judgment should be made about your child's selections. If unusual combinations are selected consistently, you might ask whether that combination has ever been served at home, and why, or why not?
6. Prepare one of the selected meals during the next weekend and allow your child to make the necessary purchases with you. He or she can also help with part of the meal preparation.
7. For variation, give your child an "adequate diet" chart, such as the one below, to use as a guide in planning the meals. Talk about the possible influence of good nutrition on the total cost of meals for a weekend.

Meat Group	Vegetable/Fruit Group	Bread/Cereal Group
2 or more	4 or more	4 or more

Milk Products Group
Children 1–8: 2 to 3
Children 9–12: 3 or more
Teenagers: 4 or more
Adults: 2 or more

Comment

This activity gives a child first-hand experience with a common budget area—meal planning—and the subsequent actual purchase of items for one meal reinforces the very real cost of feeding a family.

Evaluation

1. How did your child handle the task of "buying" food for a weekend?
2. Was he or she able to make the transition from a make-believe buying situation to a real one?
3. How did you and your child enjoy working together?

PLUMBING REPAIRS

Younger Child—Why Do Things Go Wrong?

Materials: plunger; piece of garden hose; coat hanger; scraps of paper or facial tissue

1. Ask your child to come with you to watch what you do with the drain.
2. Explain that there is something blocking the drain, keeping the water from moving freely.
3. Show him or her a plunger (which you identify) and demonstrate how it is used.

4. If your child wants to hold on to the plunger while you work it, allow him or her to do so while feeling the motion of the plunger.
5. When the plunger begins to work, show your child that the water drains freely again and that the object is repaired.
6. After this, take the old piece of garden hose and stuff it with pieces of paper or facial tissue.
7. Pour water in one end, showing your child that the water cannot run through to the other end.
8. With a straightened coat hanger, have your child try to push the tissue or paper through the hose to the opposite end. After a while, flush water through the hose to see whether it is clear.

Comment

Children are naturally inquisitive. They enjoy asking questions and understanding the reasons objects break or need fixing. Although your child may not be able to repair the household item, he or she can begin to understand what happens when things do become nonfunctional and what can be done so they can become functional once again. This activity is to be done when you actually have a stopped-up drain. It not only allows the child to be part of a household task but is an excellent learning experience, demonstrating the principle of repair. It becomes more of a relationship-building activity as you talk together about what is happening.

Evaluation

1. How did your child enjoy taking part in the task?
2. What was his or her level of interest during the activity?
3. How did you feel about the time spent with your child?

Older Child—Stopped-up Drain

Materials: plumber's snake (optional); plunger

1. Ask your child to get the plunger.

2. Allow him or her to use it and begin trying to unstop the drain. Do not demonstrate or offer help now.
3. Praise your child as he or she uses the plunger. Now is the time to offer helpful hints if necessary.
4. If the plunger is not working, and you have a "snake," ask your child to try to use that (again, reassure him or her occasionally).

Comment

This is a good learning situation. Your child is building specific skills in household repair and is also becoming aware of the responsibilities associated with family life.

Evaluation
1. How did your child respond to assuming this responsibility?
2. What were your reactions as your child assumed the responsibility?
3. What were your impressions about the nature of your interaction with your child?

THE WORLD OF WORK

WORK

Younger Child—How I Do My Work

Materials: object(s) used in your work

1. Tell your child about an occasion when you used a certain object in your work. Then demonstrate its use. Examples:
   a. Writer (pen and paper). "I sit down and use my imagination [or "think hard"] and when I have an

idea, I write it down." Sit and think and then write down some idea and read it to your child. Have your child think quietly for a minute and then tell you an idea. Write it down and read it back to him or her.

b. Secretary (typed page with two or three mistakes, a bottle of correction fluid, and the original handwritten page). "This is something Ms. Smith needed to have typed. I typed her words as I read them. When I got to the bottom of the page, there were two mistakes, here and here. This is how I correct a mistake." Demonstrate. "Now I can retype those words."

c. Teacher (science experiment, ditto sheet, or lecture notes). "This is one of the things I will share with my students tomorrow. This is what I will do . . ."

d. Draftsman (T-square and rendering of a building). "Today I was helping Mr. Brown with a picture to show how this building would look if the bricks (siding, etc.) were taken away. I used this T-square to draw where the floor and the wall would meet. Show me where that is here in our living room. Here is how I drew it for Mr. Brown."

2. After your demonstration, ask your child if he or she would like to pretend to be you. If not, perhaps your child will tell you about what he or she has just observed. Later on, he or she may pretend—with you, or alone.

3. Ask your child to show you how he or she used some object that day. Then use that object yourself.

Comment

For young children the phrase "going to work" has no real meaning, except that it separates them from their parent(s). Explained by brief demonstrations of one job segment at a time, the world of work is given some meaning. Through later make-believe, your child can incorporate a new task into his or her experience.

Evaluation

1. Did your child understand the demonstration? If not, was it presented at his or her level? Is this a type of activity that is difficult for your child to grasp?
2. Did you feel at ease in demonstrating? Did your child seem at ease in trying to repeat your actions?
3. What attitude do you have about performing this part of your job? Was your child interested, or bored? Was he or she able to express these opinions openly? Was there concern for your feelings?

Older Child—Place of Work

Materials: place of work

1. Before carrying out this activity, ask yourself the following questions about your job. This will help you to describe your work and to anticipate your child's questions.

   Is your work done indoors or outdoors?

   Do you work alone or with others?

   Do you work mainly with people or with machinery?

   Does the work involve regular or irregular hours?

   Are you happy with the work you do?

2. On a non-workday (or actual workday if convenient) take your child to your place of work and demonstrate the kind of work you do. Examples:

   a. Businessman. "This is my office. Here I write reports." Show one. "I talk to clients. Yesterday, a man came in and . . ." Explain a recent transaction that took place.

   "This is the conference room. I meet here with the other people I work with. We talk about how to sell more [whatever].

   "This is my boss's office. Remember when I came home and told you all about my raise? Well, he called me into this office that day and told me about it.

"Here is the cafeteria where I eat lunch.

"Here is where my secretary works. When you call, she answers this phone and then uses this button to buzz me."

    b. Carpenter. You might start at the lumber yard and then move to the construction site. Show where the workers talk together before beginning the day's activities. "Here is the part of the [whatever structure] where I worked yesterday. This is what I helped to put together."

2. Once home, pretend you are in a certain room at your office or at your work site and ask your child to tell you what you do in that room or to pretend to be you. If conversations occur, have a pretend conversation about a real situation.

Comment

It may be easier for the older child to grasp several related parts of a job by associating them with the place where they occur.

This activity can be segmented. One day you might point out the bank where your firm does business. Point out the section of road you helped to complete recently. Point out some of the buildings where you solicit business.

Have fun with the pretending time. You might try switching roles or making up situations. Ask your child to give you background about an incident at school and then try to role-play it.

Evaluation

1. Did your child initiate questions about your work? Did you give him or her time to ask questions? Was each really listening to the other?
2. Did you or the child feel awkward about role-playing? How was the awkwardness handled?
3. Are you able to have private time at home, or do there always seem to be interruptions? Do either of you find it hard to concentrate during these private times?

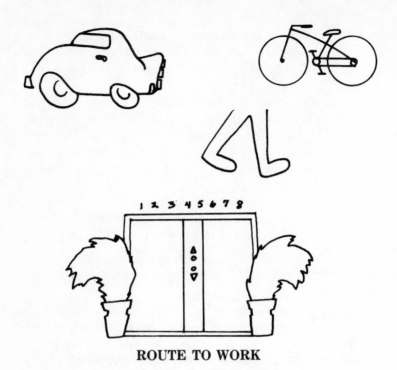

ROUTE TO WORK

Younger Child—How Does Daddy Get to Work?

Materials: butcher paper, wrapping paper, *or* plain typing paper; pen *or* magic marker; scissors

1. Ask your child how he or she gets to the grocery or to a friend's house. Talk about when to walk and when to ride in a car or bus. Ask him or her to think about all the different ways people travel from one place to another.
2. Draw a small square ☐ at each end of the sheet of paper.
3. Tell your child that the square at one end of the paper is home and that the square at the other end is where you work.
4. Ask your child how you get from home to work. As he or she tells you, place symbols on the paper in the

appropriate order. For examples of symbols, see above. Be sure to include all the methods you use to get to work, even walking to the car and taking the elevator to the proper floor.

5. Cut paper up to make a simple puzzle.
6. Take turns putting the pieces of the puzzle back together. Help each other; it's not a contest.
7. As follow-up, ask your child when he or she has used each of the methods.

Comment

This kind of activity is one way to help a younger child begin to identify with a grown-up's daily routine. The puzzle is meant to be used for fun, although sequencing can be a learning by-product. The follow-up idea is a way to help your child understand that he or she already does some of the things that you do.

Evaluation

1. Did you have fun? Did the child appear to be having a good time?
2. Was the sequencing beyond your child's cognitive level of development?
3. Did you or the child refer to the activity at a later time?

Older Child—Map Work

Materials: two street maps; fine-tipped felt pen *or* ballpoint pen; magnifying glass (optional)

1. Tell your child that together, you will use maps to draw your route to work.
2. On one of the street maps, place a dot on your home, and another dot at your place of employment. Give this map to your child.
3. Keep the second map, and from it, give directions, street by street. Example: "Start at our house and follow Main Street to 5th Street." Your child finds the street on his or her map and draws a line from one point to the next. (You may wish to use a magnifying

glass.) Find the streets together, if your child is having difficulty. Continue until the entire route is marked.
4. Go over the entire route again with your child, taking turns at each new street.
5. As a follow-up, repeat the activity, but let your child see how much he or she can find and mark by him- or herself. Perhaps you could write the directions on a piece of paper.
6. As another follow-up, you could describe some of the sights along the route.
7. You could also use the same map and draw your child's route from home to school, or to some favorite place such as the "Y," church, or music lessons.

Comment

This is a common kind of map study, one in which your child may already have participated at school. The point here is to help him or her "tune in" to part of your daily routine. It is a way to say that you think your child is important and that you want to share. The last follow-up activity is evidence that you consider his or her daily activities important, too.

Evaluation
1. Did you and the child enjoy the activity? or was it seen as a chore?
2. Was each of you the leader and the follower at different times during the activity?

CAREER AWARENESS

Younger Child—Deciding on a Job

Materials: family album; old magazines; scissors; notebook paper; tape; pencil; notebook

1. Browse through the picture album and name the family members. Name the specific jobs of immediate and extended-family members and friends. Point out that men and women also perform job tasks in the home.

2. After several pages, turn back and ask the child to repeat as many jobs as he or she can remember. Give hints if your child has difficulty.
3. As a follow-up, suggest to your child that you look for magazine pictures of people working at jobs. Let your child cut out his or her favorite pictures and tape them to notebook paper. Write the name of the occupation at the bottom of the page.
4. Place the pages of illustrations in a notebook.
5. Label the book "My Book of Careers," with your child's name.
6. As another follow-up activity, allow your child to pretend to work at the occupation of either a relative or a character from the magazine.

Comment

The purpose of this activity is to introduce a young child to the world of careers. A primary method of illustrating the world of work is to examine the jobs held by various family members. Construction of the personal notebook offers your child an exercise in cutting and taping, and practice in associating words with pictures. You might use short sentences to describe what the career person is doing in the picture. Example: "The carpenter hammers the nail."

Evaluation

1. What types of occupations did your child select for the notebook? Are the jobs sex-stereotyped? Are they similar to, or different from the work you do?
2. Was your child aware of the occupations of friends and members of the family?
3. Do you feel that you and the child were listening to each other?

Older Child—Exploring Careers

Materials: resource books on careers; paper; pencil; family album

1. Browse through a family album. Discuss the jobs of members of the immediate and the extended family, and jobs of friends. Emphasize the concept that tasks in the home constitute the workload of the career homemaker.
2. Ask your child if he or she has thought about future choices of occupation. Without being judgmental, allow him or her to talk about possibilities.
3. Share your personal experience in choosing a career. Cite examples of people who changed careers at least once during their lives.
4. Suggest a trip to the library to research a number of occupations suggested by your child. Most libraries have a telephone information service which you could use to prepare ahead of time for the visit. Biographies of famous people and handbooks on occupations are good sources.
5. When you arrive at the library, ask the librarian for help. As you and your child read about various

careers, write down answers to questions such as these:

Where does a person in this occupation work?

How much training is involved?

What would be exciting or dull about this job?

Is the work done mainly with tools, with people, or by writing?

Other interesting information.

If your child is a nonreader or a poor reader, check with the audio-visual department of your library for film strips, records, and so on that may give similar information.

6. Use the written information to help you visualize and discuss a variety of careers. Try to help your child understand the interdependence of occupations and gain an appreciation of people who perform important tasks, even though they may be jobs in which your child is not interested.

Comment

This experience fosters your child's sense of self-reliance concerning his or her acquisition of information. Knowledge about changes of mind, choices in general, and possible career changes allows a child to identify with the challenge of careers. Your personal disclosure about your career choice, or your career-choice dilemma, or the circumstances that led you to accept a job simply because it was available and you needed employment can be useful. This activity can also aid in developing a sense of apreciation and understanding of people who have different kinds of jobs.

Evaluation

1. Is your child interested in researching possible careers?
2. Did your child react to your disclosure?
3. Are you able to talk about careers without encouraging or discouraging him or her from your occupation?
4. Does this kind of activity seem to be bringing the two of you closer together?

5. Did your child seem awed by, or snobbish about certain types of jobs? How did you handle this?

COOPERATION AT WORK

Younger Child—Working Together

Materials: stapler; paper to be stapled; crayons (optional)

1. Place several sheets of paper in front of your child and say that you would like some help in getting the papers ready to staple.
2. Tell your child that this is one part of the work you do at the office (or is similar to some jobs you do) and something with which you would like some help. If you do not actually have a stapling task to complete as part of your job, make one up for this activity. For example, you could draw apples, pears, grapes, and other fruit on separate sheets of paper—three sheets with apples, three with pears, three with grapes, and so on.
3. Ask your child to separate the papers into piles of apples, pears, grapes (or whatever might actually need to be stapled together).
4. Show your child how to take a sheet from each pile and place it with the others until each set of fruit is complete.
5. Let your child make the sets and hand them to you for stapling.
6. Depending on the age and skill of your child, he or she might take a turn at stapling.
7. Your child might share copies of the stapled work with other members of the family.

Comment

Children enjoy helping with tasks. In this case, you should be certain to inform your child that this is just one of the tasks that make up the daily routines in many offices. By working together, the idea of cooperation is also illustrated. The important part of this activity should be the dialogue, stressing how this task is related to other tasks and that working together is useful in finishing the job.

Evaluation
1. Was your child able to comprehend the work that needed to be done?
2. Do you think your child understood the idea of cooperation in this activity?
3. How did you and your child enjoy working together?

Older Child—Team Effort

Materials: store, office, or factory where some product is made

1. Take a tour with the child of some store, office, or factory where some tangible item is made. This could range from a promotional tour offered by a factory, to a tour of a bakery arranged by personal request, to a visit to a family-run farm. The choice depends on what you and your child are interested in *and* what is available.
2. Prior to the tour, suggest that you both give special attention to ways the people there work together to complete the final product.
3. After the tour, compare your findings.
4. Ask your child to try to think of a recent time when he or she cooperated on some school, Scout, or other project.
5. Give an example of the way you cooperate in your work. Stress the fact that your child is learning the same skill (cooperation) that you use again and again in making a living.
6. As a follow-up, role-play or review together either the tour or some other experience you have shared.
7. If your own work involves the production of some tangible item, try to arrange a trip there. Allow your

child to try some of the tasks involved, if possible. Stress the importance of cooperation in your particular work setting. Show how the people who work there carry out specific tasks to get the overall job done.

Comment

This is a much more complex activity than the one for a younger child. It helps to demonstrate in a somewhat abstract fashion the interdependence of people's roles in a work setting. By observing those roles and allowing an older child the opportunity to play such a role, he or she can understand how the individual parts contribute to the whole project or product. This activity can be applied to a variety of settings. The tour obviously can serve a number of purposes, in addition to stressing the idea of cooperation.

Evaluation

1. How often do you and your child cooperate on an activity?
2. How did you get your child to participate in a role? Was it difficult for your child to think of his or her own examples?
3. Could your child relate to the skills that the people you saw needed in order to complete the whole project?

RULES AND CONSEQUENCES

Younger Child—Our Rules

Materials: this book

1. Read your child this story or tell it from memory:
    Once upon a time there were four bears: Mike, the father; Mindy, the mother; John, the son; and Jane, the daughter. They lived in the forest, in a house at the foot of a tree.

    Each of the children had toys. John enjoyed his blocks, and Jane liked to hammer pieces of wood. Sometimes Jane and John played alone with their own toys. At other times, John and Jane played together.

Sometimes they would fight. If they yelled at each other, their father and mother might say, "Please use your inside (quiet) voices."

One day, John and Jane were so angry with each other that John threw a block at Jane. Luckily, he missed. But mother bear said, "It is not a choice to throw blocks. Use words to tell your sister you are angry."

John said, "But she was hitting me."

Mother said to Jane, "It is not a choice to hit someone when you are angry. You can use words."

Jane said, "I told John not to run in the house and he called me Dumb-dumb."

Father said, "Calling names is not a choice. Calling names hurts feelings. Try to get along, or both of you will have to be sent to your rooms."

John and Jane listened to their parents. Rules are important to know. Remember to listen to the rules at your house.

2. Ask your child to tell you one of the rules from the story.
3. Ask what would happen if Jane or John broke the rule.
4. Ask your child to name a rule he or she is to follow. (If you normally use another word for *rule*, such as *direction* or *things to remember*, use the same phrase during this activity.)
5. Ask what could happen if the rule is broken. (Examples: If you leave gate open, dog runs away; grab toy from another child, spend time out in "thinking chair"; don't try each food at mealtime, no dessert.)
6. Talk about why the rule is important. (Examples: dog would be lost; kindness makes others happy and gives us a good feeling inside; different kinds of food help our bodies stay healthy.) Don't be surprised if it takes a long time for your child to make this connection; it is a difficult concept for young children.
7. Repeat steps 3–5 with various rules occasionally, until

you feel that your child realizes what the rules are and why they are important.

8. Following a conversation about one of your child's rules, tell him or her that in your job you have some rules to follow and ask if he or she can think of what they might be. Together you can name rules such as being on time, remembering instructions, putting tools away at the end of the day.

9. At a later time, take turns naming rules each of you must follow. Talk together about what could happen if you did not follow one of your rules. (Examples: If you do not put tools away, they could rust or be stolen; are not at work on time, rest of assembly line cannot begin work; forget instructions to order paper, report not ready on time.)

10. As a follow-up, help your child understand that sometimes you do not like to follow all the rules, but you know that others are depending on you. If you don't do your part, people may still like you as a person, but they won't like working with you, and you might lose your job.

11. Depending on the particular child and the stage of your relationship, you could talk about the way each of you feels when you are reprimanded for forgetting or for breaking a rule.

Comment

The concept of consequence is difficult for many young children to understand. Don't be discouraged if you can complete only steps 1—5 of this activity. The point is to help your child understand that rules and consequences are part of your work, just as they are part of your child's life. People depend upon one another, and you want to do your part. *Avoid* the notion that not keeping a rule makes you or your child bad. *Don't* dwell on the idea that you would lose your job if you broke a rule; young children have keen imaginations.

Evaluation

1. Did you allow your child time to think about the rules

and consequences, or did you supply the responses yourself?

2. Does your child seem to be aware of the reasons for your family's rules?

3. Do you feel that you are getting the idea across that both you and your child are important and lovable, even though you may break a rule occasionally?

Older Child—Rules of the Game

Materials: paper and pencil (optional)

This activity might take place after enjoying some table game, after being spectators or participants at a sporting event, or during casual conversation. It would be wise to refrain from such a conversation immediately after a rule infraction. The attempt at conversation at that time might be interpreted as "preaching."

1. Ask what it would have been like if there had been no rules for the game just completed. You might discuss the purpose of certain rules, or your opinion of the umpire's calls.

2. Continue by telling about some rule, written or unwritten, that you find hard to follow at your work, or one that you think is a very good rule.

3. Invite your child to do the same with some rule at school or at home.

4. As a follow-up, you and your child can make a verbal or written list of good rules at your place of work and at your child's school or at home. Talk about why you each think they are good rules. Do the same for rules you do not like to follow. Discuss whether the rules might be necessary, even though you do not like them.

Comment

Children need to know that there are good reasons for rules—that they are not simply nuisances imposed upon them by adults. It may help if your child realizes that you also have rules and that sometimes you are not pleased about following them. At an age when peers are increasingly important role models for youngsters, your ability to share similar experiences is advantageous to your relationship.

Evaluation

1. Were you and your child able to accept each other's opinions without being judgmental?
2. Did each of you give the other your attention? Could you each repeat the ideas of the other? (This is a good test.)
3. How does your child perceive and understand the rules enforced at home, or when he or she is with you (if you are not in the same household)?

DEVELOPING WORK SKILLS

Younger Child—Identifying Tools of the Trade

Materials: tools used in your work

1. Plan a game with your child (a pretend game or a simple card game like Go Fish). Allow him or her to select the game. Introduce the idea that your child has become better at playing this game. Example: "You know, Becky, you have learned how to play Fish very well." Add the idea that all people must practice their work (job-related or home-related) so that they can learn how to do things better.
2. Invite your child to look at some of the implements you use in your work. Identify each by its name, allowing your child to repeat the name and to handle the tool (if safe to do so). If you do not have implements available away from your place of work, describe or find pictures of such implements or pieces of machinery and tell your child their names. Use written words with the pictures to build the association between the written word and the object.

    If you work in teaching, management, counseling, sales—work that is mainly involved with people—

your approach will be different. Young children need concrete examples. For instance, if you are a teacher or counselor, you might show your child books that help you learn how to help people. If you are a salesperson, you might talk about all the items you sell and how important it is for you to know the *stock* (teach that word) and where each item is located.

3. Put the tools in a paper bag or lean them against a wall. Allow your child to pick out a tool and identify it by name. When there is an incorrect response, tell the correct name and suggest trying again.

   If you only described the implements or pieces of machinery, play a guessing game with your child: "I'm thinking of something that . . ." Take turns, so that you each have a chance to guess and to describe. This will also identify any confusion your child may have about the names of the pieces of machinery and how they are used.

   If you work mainly with people, you could use building blocks to represent your schooling—elementary school, high school, sales training, trial period, periodic sales meetings, and so on. Build a tower as you tell about each level. Then let your child build the tower and tell about your training.

4. Tell how you learned to use the implement (or training) and how you improved by practicing. You might tell it as a story, if your child enjoys stories and you enjoy storytelling.

5. Ask about something the child is practicing in order to become more skillful. (Examples: eating with an adult spoon, dressing alone, tracing, etc.)

Comment

Part of any job training is learning about the "tools of the trade," so to speak. Identification of objects you use in your work is one of the first steps in arousing your child's interest in what you do. Your child can better understand the need to practice if you relate some skill that he or she is learning.

Evaluation

1. How did you feel about explaining the different implements to your child?
2. Was your child able to learn the names of the tools?
3. Were you aware of a skill your child is learning?
4. What ways can you think of to reinforce the idea of practice?

Older Child—A Project

Materials: tools used in your work

1. This activity provides an opportunity for your child to practice using tools or to pretend a work situation. Here you can stress the idea that practice helps people improve at jobs.
2. Let your child begin to experiment (under your supervision) with the implements he or she has been able to identify. This may be done at home or at your place of work.

3. If your work involves dealing with the public—selling, counseling, management, teaching—your child can practice talking with you to develop his or her communication skills. For example, create a seller-buyer situation in which your child practices selling you the products you normally sell on your job (or dealing with management situations you sometimes face).

4. Ask your child what tools or job he or she might be interested in learning about, perhaps to use later in making a living. If possible, give him or her a chance to observe or use the tool (or to watch a person provide the service).

Comment

Job training involves practicing the routines and procedures of a job. Your child needs to realize that becoming competent at anything involves continual practice. This is a concept that builds self-confidence as well as specific skills.

Evaluation

1. Was your child able to make the transition from understanding the use of the tools to actually working with them?

2. Was this activity adaptable to your work? How did you modify it? Are you getting better at introducing your own innovations?

3. How could this activity be applied to other areas of your child's life?

4. Was there positive interaction between you?

5. Did your child express an interest in other tools or jobs? Can you help find out about those tools or jobs?

ATTITUDES ABOUT WORK

Younger Child—Overhearing Adult Conversations

Materials: none

At the end of an adult conversation about your work which your child has overheard, ask your child to tell you what was discussed. This will at least clarify any misunderstanding. You may need to review the conversation in simpler terms. Conversation topics might include:

    problems or prospects of career advancement

    physical surroundings at work

    fringe benefits of the job, such as breaks, lunchroom facilities, holidays

    compensation for work accomplished

    interaction with co-workers—joint projects, hierarchy relationships, social activities, or conflicts

    satisfaction or dissatisfaction with content and scope of work.

Comment

It is almost inevitable that your child will overhear discussions of events, people, and attitudes relating to your work. Just as you feel it is important to hear about your child's activities and to take time to understand his or her feelings, your children are interested in and want to understand your feelings about your work. In the process of conversation, you will be teaching appropriate (we hope) attitudes about work, controversies, and co-workers, whether they are subordinates, supervisors, or at the same job level.

Evaluation

1. Were you able to discuss conflict situations so as to show your child that you can respect persons even though you disagree with their behavior or ideas? (It takes young children a *long* time to accomplish this same regard for others; even many adults have not yet accomplished this feat.)
2. Was your child surprised to be included in an "adult" topic? Was he or she interested, or bored? (Remember that children learn to become interested in others as they experience others' interest in them.)
3. What lesson is your child learning from you about responsibility? (The care with which your child picks

up toys may reflect the way you talk about doing your own work.)

Older Child—Our Associates

Materials: tablet or typing paper; pen or pencil

See conversation topics mentioned in the younger child activity.

1. At the end of an adult conversation about any of those topics which your child has overheard, ask your child to explain in his or her own words what you were talking about.
2. Make a mental or written chart comparing your co-workers to persons in your child's environment. (Examples: your supervisor = child's teacher; head of your organization = principal of child's school; co-worker/friend = child's playmate.) This chart can be the framework for discussion about feelings toward those persons.
3. Keep an "attitude" diary for a specified period of time. Each of you chooses a person in your work or school environment. Then, each day for 10 working days (or whatever length of time you have chosen), take a few minutes to tell each other your current feelings about those persons. You might like to make two calendars, one for each of you, and draw faces every day to describe your feelings toward those persons. After the specified period of time, repeat the procedure occasionally.
4. As a follow-up activity, you could each talk about something that could improve the relationships or maintain them; or perhaps the conversation could center on whether to continue the relationships at all.
5. During the evening meal, or at some other convenient time, each member of the family (or you and one child,

if that is better for your schedule) can tell what he or she enjoyed most during that day, and why. Choices should be accepted, rather than evaluated.

Comment

This is a good exercise in mutual respect. Also, since we are often inclined to focus on negative events, the family-time activity is one way to redirect our attention and encourage a positive orientation toward life.

Activity 5 may or may not relate to the world of work (school, or work at home) depending on the responses of the family members. If work or school are never mentioned by certain family members, this might indicate a basic dissatisfaction that could be discussed at another time.

Evaluation

1. Do you feel that you and your child were both honest about your feelings toward associates?
2. Are you growing in your ability to work toward better relationships with those with whom you may have occasional conflicts?
3. Do you appreciate your good relationships and try to think of ways to make them even better?

MEDIA CAREERS

Younger Child—TV Teaches Careers

Materials: television set; paper; crayons (Note: This activity can also be based on a movie.)

1. Allow your child to select his or her favorite program on television.
2. View the show together.
3. After the program, ask your child to tell you what the story was about.
4. Together, sketch pictures of the characters portrayed in the program. (Don't be embarrassed to use stick figures.)
5. Talk about the actions of the characters.

6. Focus on the job-related actions in your drawings. Ask which of those your child would enjoy doing, and which are better simply to watch on TV.
7. Ask your child what he or she would like to be when grown.

Comment

Children love to watch superheroes on television and in movies, and these models often offer the viewer subtle messages concerning careers. Your interaction with your child can enhance his or her understanding—not only of careers, but of the values and information the show portrays.

Evaluation

1. Did your child report a favorite occupation?
2. Did your child exhibit knowledge of the characteristics of his or her favorite characters? favorite occupations?

Older Child—Movies Teach Careers

Materials: current newspaper (Note: This activity can also be based on a TV show.)

1. Ask your child if he or she enjoys going to the movies.
2. Select a film that is acceptable to both of you. You might begin by saying that you have "veto power," explaining what that means. If there is disagreement about the choice of film, discuss the meaning of movie ratings (G, PG, R, X).
3. After viewing the film, talk about the plot and the motivations of the characters.
4. Relate the story to the city or town where you live. For example, could the story have happened where you live? Did it take place in the past, present, or future? What was your town like in the past? or What will it be like in the future?
5. Talk about the jobs of the characters in the movie. Compare their occupations with jobs of people in your locale.

Comment

Older children can discuss the occupations of media characters in more detail than younger children can. Together, you can talk about occupations of real people in your neighborhood and the values and ideas portrayed in the movie. Focus on the different types of jobs found in cities and in the country. Additionally, you might consider discussing the idea that many things your child does now will help him or her in a future job. For example, when handing in school assignments, he or she learns about punctuality and quality of work; when caring for clothing, learns about appearance and job-required dress; when writing school papers, learns communication skills and organization of thought.

Evaluation

1. Did your child understand the plot and occupations?
2. Did your child know five occupations found in your city?
3. Is your child interested in thinking about a future career?

FOR LEISURE TIME

CARPENTRY

Younger Child—Toy Shelves

Materials: 2 melon or orange crates; 4 to 6 2½" or 3" nails; 12 to 16 1" nails; sheet of ¼" plywood 4' x 4'; light-weight hammer; saw; pencil; yardstick

In this activity, you will be making a set of shelves from two wooden crates, one placed lengthways on top of the other. Before the crates are nailed together, pieces of

plywood will be cut and placed on the "floor" of the bottom crate, on the floor of the top crate, and on the top of the top crate.

1. Lay one crate on its long side, with the opening facing sideways. Place the other crate on top in the same position. Ask your child to pretend that the top, the middle, and the bottom are solid pieces of wood, rather than slats. Ask your child to think what the boxes could be used for. Example: shelves for dishes or toys.
2. Measure the *inside* length and depth of a crate. Your child may steady the yardstick.
3. Saw 2 pieces of plywood to fit those dimensions. Your child may steady the yardstick, steady the pieces of wood, or even hold the saw *with you* if you think that is safe.
4. While the crates are lying on their sides, let your child slide a piece of plywood into each one. When they are

in place, nail them to the bottoms of the crates, using 4 nails for each. Your child can hold the hammer with you *or* you can start the nail and then give your child a turn at hammering. (If you do this, buy a few extra nails in case some get bent.) When completed, you will have serviceable shelves.

5. Measure the *outside* length and width of the long side of a crate.
6. Measure and saw one piece of plywood to fit those dimensions.
7. Place the plywood on the outside of a crate to form the top of the cupboard. Nail into place.
8. Together, lift the crate with the plywood top onto the bottom crate. Position evenly. Using the longer nails, nail the two crates together where the two ends are indented.
9. Put away all tools. (Tool boxes have locks and can be stored out of your child's reach.)
10. Decide where the new furniture is to be used and put it in place.
11. Place books, dishes, etc., on the shelves.
12. As a follow-up, practice hammering nails into soft plywood.
13. Think of other ways discards—boxes, coffee cans, etc.—could be put to good use.
14. As another follow-up, cut pictures of carpentry tools from a catalog, glue them onto pieces of paper, and use them as flashcards, so that your child can learn the names of some of the more common tools.

Comment

In this activity, you and your child are using tools that can be part of a hobby for you. Your child is gaining experience with the tools and with the process followed when working on a carpentry project. And together, you are creating something useful for your child. This is also an example of using materials discarded by others to create something of worth. You might use this activity as an occasional reminder to you both to look for creative possibilities in everyday objects.

As you build the shelves, ask where the wood and the nails came from. Be aware that you are conserving natural resources when you use products for more than one purpose. A follow-up might be a nature walk, pointing out the young saplings, gathering seeds to indicate the stages of growth, and talking about the length of time it takes a tree to grow big enough to be used to make various things.

Evaluation
1. Did you think to tell your child that it was more fun to do this project with him or her than alone? Was it, in fact, enjoyable to build together?
2. Are you too much of a perfectionist, bossy, or do you praise every attempt? (Was praise deserved when given?)
3. Did your child have the patience to learn to use the tools correctly?

Older Child—Toy Shelves

Materials: same as for younger child

1.—14. Same as for younger child. Depending on the cognitive level and skill with tools, your child can perform the measuring, sawing, and hammering with or without assistance from you.
15. As another follow-up, open your toolbox and show the tools one by one. Then let your child pick up and name as many tools as possible. Do this until your child knows all the tools.

Comment
The shelves may be for your child or they could be a gift for a younger child. In that case, there would be the satisfaction of making a gift for another. Use your imagination: A crate on its end with plywood on the top could be a stove with painted-on electric or gas elements; a crate could be a cart, if wheels were attached. The use of free material to create

useful toys and other objects can aid the family's financial state by providing gifts that will be cherished and enjoyed when made by you for your child or by one child for another.

Evaluation

Same as for younger child.

COMMUNITY INVOLVEMENT

Younger Child—Helping Out

Materials: paper and pencil

1. Visit an animal shelter. (A preschool or elementary school visit by an animal shelter employee is common in many localities. You might check the school schedule to see if such a visit is planned and arrange for your personal visit following the presentation.) Have an employee explain how the shelter helps prevent cruelty to animals.

2. Make a point of picking up trash and disposing of it in garbage cans, or in a sack you keep in the car, or one that you take with you when going for a walk. Say something like, "I'm picking up this trash to help keep our city clean. I like this city and I want to help make it look nice." Make this a habit so that eventually your child throws trash in cans on his or her own or gets a small sack from the cupboard before taking a walk.

3. Tell your child when you are going to some civic meeting. Let him or her learn the name of the organization(s). Tell your child, in general terms, what the organization does. Examples:

   a. "I am going to the Shriners meeting tonight. The Shriners earn money to help people who have been burned. The Shriners have a special hospital for people from all over the country who have had bad burns. The next thing we will do to raise money is (kind of project). Tonight I will find out what part I will have in the project."

   b. "Tonight there is a meeting of the city council (or neighborhood organization, planning commission, school board, state legislature). I am going to the meeting because I am interested (worried, concerned) about (whatever local issue it might be). I want to find out what other people think, and maybe I will have a chance to say what I think. I want to help our representatives make good decisions." Or if you are a representative in an organization, go over the agenda items with your child before going to the meeting.

   c. "The education committee is meeting at church this evening. We will talk about Sunday school classes for the summer and also about Bible school. Would you like to tell me some things you liked (or didn't like) about last year's classes, so that I can keep them in mind when we make our plans this evening?"

4. As a follow-up to the examples in step 3:
   a. Take your child to the planned event. Let your child stay with you if you are ticket taker or have any such task that would allow for a young spectator.
   b. Let your child know the agenda items that were used and the decisions that were reached, if any.
   c. As the program unfolds in the future, refer to the meeting(s) you had told him or her about when the plans were being made. The point is to illustrate something tangible from a series of meetings.
5. Through discussion, you can learn whether your child understands the meaning of your civic involvement. You can stress that you are involved because you care about others and that you want your town (church, etc.) to be the best it can be.
6. Let your child tell you about some event at school or at home or with friends. Then try to tell your child about the event in your own words, to be sure you understand the particular situation that was significant for him or her.
7. Ask your child if there is something he or she particularly enjoys about your town. It might be the schoolyard, the park system, the band in the club down the street that plays more softly now. Together, compose a letter of thanks to the appropriate organization. If your child has trouble thinking of something he or she likes, take a bus ride, or walk, or drive, and point out some municipal services.
8. Hold a family or group meeting. The topic should be of importance to the family and one in which the child can be involved, even in a limited way. Some possibilities:
   Should we get a new roof?
   Convert the attic into a bedroom?
   How can we solve the problem of dogs running loose in the neighborhood?

Comment

This activity will introduce the child to the idea that one cares for others by being a responsible citizen (church member, etc.). The specific activities your child carries out are as important as his or her understanding of your community involvement. It may be that at some time in the past it has been necessary for you to depend on the goodwill of some civic organization. If so, let your child know that anyone might need special help at times, and tell about the time when you did. This is a way to help your child respect all people, without regard to economic or physical circumstance. A sense of community involvement is directly related to the level of family involvement in solving problems.

Evaluation

1. How comfortable were you in talking about ways you are involved in your community? Did you find yourself being embarrassed, condescending, or pompous?
2. What is your child's attitude toward picking up trash, thanking public servants, planning for better programs? As he or she grows, so should the awareness and acceptance of his or her own responsibility.
3. Did you listen to the narration of your child's activity as well as he or she listened to yours?

Older Child—Helping Out

Materials: paper and pen

1.—6. Same as for younger child. You can use more mature language, because this is an older child. Remember that your child will be learning *your* attitudes as you share with him or her, so be responsible.
7. If your child has the attention span and would be permitted to attend, take him or her to an actual meeting. On the way home, and also at a later time, let your child ask questions so that you can be sure he or she understood what was happening. If you had certain feelings during a particular part of the meeting

let your child know how you felt. Meetings *can* be boring or exciting, or make one angry, disgusted, etc.

8. If, at some point, your child complains about some municipal service (no bus route where one is needed, ruts in the street that make it hard to ride a bike, no crosswalk in the middle of the block at the school or park, etc.), ask if he or she can think of a way the situation might be changed. The possibility that it actually could be changed may be surprising to a child. Listen to his or her suggestions. Ideas to consider: an individual letter, a letter from a whole class at school, a visit to the person in charge, a neighborhood petition, a consultation with a member of the city council. It will be your job to see that the action taken is handled tactfully. More than one draft of a letter or one rehearsal of a meeting with an official might be useful. Carry through with your child's concern.

9. Your child may get an idea for service after hearing you talk about service organizations or church meetings. Listen to the ideas and, together, think of ways to utilize his or her interest. If your child belongs to some group such as the "Y," Scouts, a children's choir, Sunday school class, etc., find out together if the group has any service projects. If so, be sure to participate. If not, you and your child may wish to be the ones to initiate some helping activity.

Comment
Same as for younger child.

Evaluation
Same as for younger child.

CB/SHORT-WAVE RADIO

Younger Child—Pretend Conversations

Materials: (all optional) CB or short-wave equipment; heavy string; scissors; 2 clean empty tin cans; hammer; nail

1. Over a period of time, allow your child to observe your use of the equipment and, one by one, learn the phrases commonly used in sending and receiving messages. Be sure to tell your child what the expressions mean.

2. Play a game. If you have an extension phone, each of you can use a receiver. Pretend you are using the CB or short wave and carry on a mock conversation. If you do not have an extension phone, have your child hide behind a couch, chair, or bed. Take turns initiating the conversation.

3. Make a two-way telephone, if there is interest on *both* your parts. Make a hole in the middle of the closed end of each tin can by hammering the point of the nail through it. Cut a piece of string long enough to reach from one room to another. Push one end of the string through the hole in one can, and make a knot on the inside of the can. Repeat with the other end of the string and the other tin can.

4. You and your child each take a can and place yourselves in different rooms. Hold the string taut, taking care that it does not touch any object. If it does, the sound will stop where it touches. Take turns speaking into and listening through the open ends of the cans. Use the expressions common to CB or short-wave communication.

Comment

This kind of activity allows your child to enter your adult world. You don't need any particular props, except a skill you already have. The object is to share something you enjoy with your child and, in so doing, let your child know that you think he or she is special enough to share this special hobby.

Evaluation

1. Did your child realize that he or she was gaining skill in a hobby that you enjoy?
2. Are you satisfied with the patience you displayed in teaching your child the common expressions?
3. Did you have some silly conversations just for fun, or was the activity seen as a serious task only?

Older Child—Codes

Materials: paper; pen or pencil; 3 X 5 cards

1. Same as younger child.
2. Bring home from the library (or visit the library together and bring home) books showing various codes. The codes could be the flag signals used by the coast guard, the flag positions used at airports to direct airplanes, etc. Decide which kind of code would appeal most to *both* of you, or you might choose more than one, for comparison.
3. Choose several expressions that are common at your home (or when you are together, if you are not a family member). Together, think of pictures or letter symbols to represent those expressions.

Examples:

in a minute

time for dinner

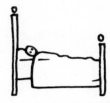

bedtime

4. Draw one symbol on each 3 X 5 card. For fun, show each other the symbol instead of speaking the words when they come up in conversation.
5. If there is interest, make up a symbol to represent each letter of the alphabet. Each of you can keep a copy of the code. Examples:
   A = ⊡
   B = ♡
   Z = ⊗
6. Occasionally, you can leave coded messages for each other in lunchboxes, on pillows, on dinner plates, etc.

Comment

This activity allows you to share common CB and short-wave expressions with your child. It also offers a way to use the idea of codes or special expressions to create a "language" for you to share. It's nice to have something that belongs just to the two of you and lets each of you know that you are special to the other.

Evaluation

1. Did you have a good feeling about having a special code that belongs to just you two? Do you think it was special to the child?
2. How good were your imaginations in thinking of symbols? Did you enjoy using library books for your ideas?
3. Do you think your child has a greater appreciation for the details of your hobby, and for language in general?

OUT-OF-DOORS

Younger Child—The Five Senses Outside

Materials: places to walk outdoors; items around the house

1. Smell
   a. Choose a place and time of year to walk so that various odors can be smelled. Examples: wild onion, mint, flowering shrubs, pine trees, dust, "fishy" water, freshness after rain.
   b. Tell your child you are going to take a "smelling" walk. Feel free to experience with all your senses, but concentrate on smells. At times, point out a smell. At other times, ask your child to go to some object, smell it, and tell you what it smells like.
   c. You might blindfold yourself or your child at some point, then smell something pleasant (flower, pine needles, etc.), and try to guess what you are smelling.
   d. At home, select a variety of smells. (Be sure none of the vapors is harmful!) Examples: orange, vinegar, car polish, soap, garbage can, peppermint candy. Smell each one in turn and talk about that particular smell.

e. If you are comfortable doing so, offer a brief prayer of thanks for such a variety of smells in the world, and for noses to enjoy them.

Repeat the same basic procedure (steps a–e) with each of the senses. Examples are listed under each heading.

2. Taste

Examples out-of-doors: mint leaves, grass, wild berries (*if* you are sure they are nonpoisonous), wild onion, sassafras bark.

Examples at home: lemon, salt, sugar, peppermint-flavored gum, cinnamon. Try a bite of food without salt; then add salt and taste again.

3. Touch

Examples out-of-doors: bark, moss, different grasses, flower petal, smooth and rough stones.

Examples at home: metals, glass, rough and finished woods, carpet, upholstered furniture, clothing, new and worn tennis balls, water, oil, juice.

4. Hearing

Examples out-of-doors: sound of flies, bees, birds, animals, rustle of leaves, water flowing, lawn mower, garbage truck, delivery trucks, cars, own footsteps.

Examples at home: refrigerator or furnace going on and off, clock, person walking overhead, voices expressing a variety of feelings, various appliances.

5. Sight

Examples out-of-doors: young and mature trees, homes of animals and birds, depth of water, different leaves, sunlight and shadows, flowers and other plants.

Examples at home: characteristics of persons, colors of food, size and shape of furniture, areas in light and in darkness.

Comment

Both you and your child can become increasingly aware of the stimulation provided by your senses. By paying specific attention to one at a time, you can heighten awareness of that sense. We hope this activity will help you to enjoy life more fully with *all* your senses.

Evaluation

1. Was it hard for either of you to concentrate on enjoying with a particular sense?
2. Did each of you have an opportunity to point out items of interest?
3. Do you feel that your child is gaining a sense of wonder and appreciation of his or her environment in nature and at home?
4. Did you enjoy interacting with your child during this activity?

Older Child—A Terrarium

Materials: places to walk outdoors; large widemouthed jar *or* aquarium; lid or aluminum foil; pebbles or gravel; topsoil; small woodland plants; moss; box or sack; trowel or knife

1.—5. Same as for younger child. Your explanation and the child's involvement will be more sophisticated because of age.

6. Take a walk in a wooded area, carrying the box or sack with you. As you walk, notice the *small* plants in the area. Compare them to larger species or to a mature version of the same plant.

7. At a bare spot, dig and place in the box or sack enough soil to make a layer at least 3 inches deep in the bottom of your jar or aquarium. Tree stumps that have disintegrated provide good "soil" also. As you dig the soil with the trowel or knife, recall the dead plants that have rotted to make soil that is good for growing things.

8. Lift some patches of moss by cutting under them to loosen them. Place in the box or bag. Think about the fact that the moss helps prevent erosion by providing a good ground cover.

9. Dig around the roots of several small plants and gently place them in the box or bag. Talk about differences and similarities between these plants and those that are cultivated by man.

10. If there is a stream nearby or you have a thermos with you, sprinkle water over the plants and moss you have gathered. This will keep them from drying out before they are planted.

11. Once home, cover the bottom of your jar or aquarium with gravel or pebbles.

12. Add the layer of dirt.

13. Sprinkle with water until all the dirt is moist.

14. Plant the small plants wherever you wish. Be sure to leave some room for growth.

15. Cover all the bare spots with patches of moss.

16. Water the terrarium well and cover with the lid or aluminum foil. Be sure there is a little open space in the lid so that air can circulate.

17. In a few days, water should begin to condense on the top and sides of the terrarium, thus beginning the

water cycle. (If it does not begin to condense, you may need to add more water.) Together, note how the water is used by the plants and then evaporates into the air, only to fall again as "rain." This is a reliable "miracle" of nature.

Comment

Same as for younger child. Building a small bit of nature together is one way to appreciate the woodland habitat. You are also working with living things and can grow in appreciation of the natural environment. This appreciation, in turn, can lead to a sense of responsibility for those parts of the world that can be preserved only if protected by persons like yourselves.

Evaluation

1. Same as for younger child.
2. Did you and your child seem to have a sense of wonder and appreciation for the portions of nature you were collecting?
3. How well were you able to work together to plan the design for the terrarium?

READING

Younger Child—Our Stories

Materials: paper; pen; crayons *or* fine-tipped felt pens

1. Read to your child. Make it a habit to let him or her see you read. When an event occurs that reminds you of a portion of a story, tell the child what you are reminded of. Example: "That biggest pumpkin in the pile over there reminds me of the pumpkin that was turned into a coach in the Cinderella story."
2. When you have established a routine of reading to your child, ask if he or she would like for you to make up a story. (This could happen while waiting for a baseball game to start, while riding in the bus, or whenever your child seems restless or bored.) Let

your child name a subject. Example: "Tell me about outer space . . . a crocodile . . . Valentine's Day."

3. Start with "Once upon a time . . ." and let your imagination take over. If you get stuck, ask your child what he or she thinks should happen next. The story does not need to be long or make sense.

4. When you have some free time, remember the stories you have told, as best you can, and write them down. Try to have each one typed on a separate page, with an original drawing or magazine picture to illustrate the story. Put the stories into a notebook. Title it (child's name) Stories.

5. On some holiday when gifts are presented, or at any time you think appropriate, give the collection of stories to your child. Read them over together occasionally. At times, ask your child to tell *you* one of the stories.

6. Let your child tell you a story. Write the words as he

or she dictates and then read the story back to your child. Later, have the story typed, if possible, and add others to make a collection. If you include a good illustration, your child will be able to "read" the story to you when he or she sees the illustration.

7. As a follow-up activity, help your child recall some past event while you write it down. A collection of these would introduce your child to the difference between real and imaginary stories.

Comment

This kind of activity is one way to help children understand that books are made by people. By telling stories and making books, you are promoting the idea that reading is important. Making up stories is also a good way to exercise creative abilities.

Evaluation

1. Was it hard for you or your child to make up a story?
2. How did you feel about creating a gift for your child?
3. What was your child's response when he or she received this personal gift?
4. What have you learned about your child from his or her choice of story topics?
5. Is your child's interest in reading or making up stories increasing?

Older Child—Sharing Reading Topics

Materials: encyclopedias or books; tape recorder (optional); paper and pencil

In this activity it is assumed that you have a real interest in reading and that your child has some reading skills.

1. Choose a subject. Examples: weather, astronauts, fish, particular person, etc.
2. Decide together whether you will find encyclopedia articles or books about this subject.
3. Select either encyclopedias (children's and adult) or

books (juvenile and adult) by looking at the card catalog.
4. If you have chosen encyclopedia articles:
   a. Read the articles separately.
   b. Each day, take turns telling something you learned from the articles. Retell what the other person has said to be sure you each listened carefully and understood the other.

   If you have chosen books:
   a. Read part of the books each day.
   b. Both of you can tell about the new things you have learned from the books each day. Each of you might repeat the other's information in your own words to be sure you have listened carefully and understood.
5. On occasion, read aloud to each other. Praise clarity and expression, and try to set an example by practicing these skills yourself.
6. If a tape recorder is available, each of you can record a poem or short story.
7. Play back the stories or poems. Critique yourselves on clarity and expression.
8. Handwrite, type, or tape-record a composition.
9. Present it as an unexpected gift to your child.

Comment

Sharing of reading material is a good way to learn from each other, and a common topic provides material for conversation. Reading aloud will sensitize you to the meaning and expression of the written word and to your own capacity for expressiveness. Developing a composition allows you to be imaginative and may motivate your child to try some creative writing.

Evaluation
1. How well did each of you listen to the other?
2. If you chose books, did you remember to talk about them each day? Who initiated the discussions?
3. Was it enjoyable, or embarrassing, to read aloud to

each other? Were you each able to allow the reader to self-evaluate, rather than offering your own criticism?

SPORTS

Younger Child—Viewing/Playing

Materials: children's sporting event; balls or other sports equipment

1. Watch a children's sporting event with your child.
2. Highlight the rules of the game. Points to focus on:
   Both boys and girls can play the game.
   There are rules that are enforced by an umpire or referee.
   It feels good to win, but sometimes we lose. (How does it feel to lose?)
   Sportsmanship. (Did the players shake hands after the game?)
3. Practice a skill used in a game. Examples: toss a ball back and forth (baseball), kick a ball toward one another (soccer and football), volley with a ball or birdie and two racquets (tennis, badminton, ping pong), float or bob (swimming), run short distances or around obstacles (track), knock down empty soft drink bottles with a ball (bowling), etc.
4. If you actively engage in a sport, consider allowing your child to watch you play (under someone's supervision). Perhaps he or she can help get your equipment or uniform ready. Afterward, tell your child about a part of the game you liked and a part you did not like; a time when you did well and a time when you didn't.
5. If your child is involved in a sport at this age, *go* to the events. Help him or her get the equipment and uniform ready. Listen as he or she tells about the good and the bad parts of the sport and the game.

Comment

Sports are often a popular area of interest for men. Remember that both boys and girls can be interested in sports. It is important to give them a chance to "try out" the various sports. It is good exercise for both you and your child and is often a way to practice being a good group member.

Evaluation

1. Did you focus on the idea of playing to the best of one's ability, rather than on beating someone or on winning the game?
2. Were you able to help your child experience success in playing a game in a modified way?
3. What is your attitude about being a team member? What is your child's attitude?

Older Child—Sports Heroes and Values

Materials: same as for younger child

1.—5. Same as for younger child.
6. While watching a sporting event, or in conversation, ask your child about his or her favorite player(s).
7. Look up the salaries of players in particular sports—specifically, of your child's favorite(s)—in sports magazines and daily newspapers. Look up the average salary of people in other careers (available from school guidance counselors and reference librarians).
8. Ask your child if he or she thinks that athletes are paid too much. Ask what he or she would do with that much money.
9. Look at the reference materials together. Consider the men and women in your child's family, in the neighborhood, or that he or she has heard about, and determine which ones, if any, are "heroes." Talk about what a "hero" is. Is the sports figure a more attractive model than people in other careers? Is money earned a good way to determine whether a person is a hero?

Comment

In considering this activity, you must explore your own values concerning money. It is important that you let your child explore his or her own values. The teaching aspect of this activity is in helping your child focus on the idea of heroes in general, and the way sports personalities fit those criteria.

Evaluation

1. Was your child able to see any people besides sports personalities as heroes?
2. How important is money to you? to your child?
3. Were you able to accept his or her level of materialism?
4. How does each of you define *hero?*

FRIENDS

Younger Child—What Are Friends Like?

Materials: friend of your child; crayon; paper

1. Ask your child to suggest a friend he or she would like to have over to play for a short while. Invite the child.
2. After the friend has left, ask your child to help you draw pictures of the kinds of things he or she likes most to do with that friend (or talk about it, if you both are comfortable with words).
3. Discuss with your child what he or she thinks friendship involves.
4. Talk about some of your friends and your child's other friends, and the things you enjoy doing with each of them.
5. See if your child can distinguish between those things he or she likes best about certain friends, and those things he or she does not like.
6. As a follow-up, listen to a Mr. Rogers record, or another children's record that deals with friendship. Learn the songs and refer to them when such situations arise.

Comment

It would be useful to point out that a friendship can last throughout a lifetime. Also, that sometimes friends become angry with each other, but make up later. Of course, sometimes they don't.

Evaluation

1. After the activity, did you feel that your child had a better understanding of the concept of friendship?
2. Did you share with your child your ideas about some of your friends whom the child may know?
3. Does your child understand that friends can be enjoyed differently, depending upon a particular friend's interests and capabilities?

Older Child—Improving Friendships

Materials: pencil or crayons; paper

1. On separate sheets of paper, each of you writes the name of one of your best friends. Then write two things you like about that person and one thing you would like to change.
2. Draw stick figures of yourselves. List two things you like about yourselves and one thing you would like to change.
3. Exchange papers and discuss the statements.
4. Without being judgmental, begin to discuss the first steps in making changes in yourselves and in causing a change in your friends.
5. Now imagine what you and your friends will be like in 10 years, in 20 years, at age 60, and at age 80. Answer these questions: Would you still be a good friend to have? What about the other person?

Comment

In this activity, there is mutual self-disclosure. This helps to model and to create a closeness with your child. The aim is to provide a space of safety, where there can be sharing and discovery. A second purpose is to think about ways to improve relationships with friends.

Evaluation

1. Could your child imagine his or her relationship with the friend in the future?
2. Are the relationships your child now has the kind you would like him or her to have?
3. Could you and your child see a process by which your friendships could be enhanced?
4. Were your child's statements about the relationship indicative of his or her stage of development, or were they indicative of some difficulty with social relationships?

HOBBIES

Younger Child—Collecting

Materials: paper sack; masking tape; shoe boxes, shelves, or drawers for storage; glue; construction paper or other heavy paper

1. Go for a walk with your child.
2. Take turns pointing out and naming interesting objects. Examples: "I see a tall tree with green leaves." "I see bottle caps on the sidewalk."
3. Ask your child if he or she would like to gather objects for a collection. If so, take a sack along on your next walk. (You may need to set some ground rules about the size of the items.) Show some enthusiasm for the "newly found" objects.
4. Take the objects home and glue or tape them to the paper. Label them. In this way the child learns to associate the word with the object.
5. If you have a collection, show it to your child. Talk about other kinds of collections.

Comment

Children normally enjoy collecting things, and in this activity you can also teach a little about words. If you have a collection, your child probably will enjoy the same type, but with objects of his or her own choosing.

Evaluation

1. Did your child enjoy this experience?
2. Did you talk about any other subjects during the course of the activity?
3. Did your child know the letters written on the labels? Can he or she (by the end of the fifth year) name colors?

Older Child—Who's Who *on Hobbies*

Materials: paper and pencil

1. Ask your child to tell you a little about his or her favorite hobby. Tell your child about yours. See if, together, you can name the hobbies of your friends and relatives. If you can't, ask them to tell you. If

either or both of you appear interested, you may also receive an explanation or demonstration.
2. List all the people's names on a sheet of paper. As you learn their hobbies, write them beside the names. This is a good social experience and helps to develop your child's communication skills.
3. Share this list of hobbies at a family meeting or at dinner some evening.
4. If your child is a collector, give him or her a loose-leaf notebook and some tape, or a plastic box with small storage bins (from hardware store). Occasionally, ask about and look at the collection.

Comment

Many of us become caught up in ourselves and often never learn important facts about our friends and family. Through this activity, you are helping your child understand his or her world more intimately.

Evaluation

1. Did your child show good communication skills while talking with people about their hobbies?
2. Did your child learn anything of interest while doing this activity? Did you?

TOOLS

Younger Child—How Tools Are Used

Materials: tool box or tool shed; tools; work bench (if available)

1. Explain to your child that tools must be cared for and that they must be handled correctly in order to work properly.
2. Allow your child to "work" (play) with or practice using some tools for carpentry (plumbing, car repair, horticulture, etc.). Examples:
   a. If you have a step stool with screws and bolts, let your child use the screw driver and wrench to tighten and untighten the bolts.

b. If you have wood clamps, show your child how to clamp pieces of wood together. Show him or her how two pieces of wood are glued together and held by the clamps until the glue is dry and strong.

c. Use a car wrench to loosen and tighten the bolts on the tires. (Loosen the bolts before your child practices. And be sure they are secure when you finish "playing.")

d. Dig up a few dandelions or other weeds with a weeder or garden trowel, use a roller over part of the lawn, or, together, hold the pruning shears to trim a few low bushes.

3. After your child has "worked" with the tools, inform him or her that they need to be put in their proper places in the tool box, on the work bench, or in the shed.

4. Show your child where to put the tools he or she can lift and the storage places he or she can reach, and allow your child to put some tools away. Take turns. You might make a game out of this by taking the tools out of

the tool box or off the bench and asking your child to call out the name of the tool and place it in its proper place.

5. As a follow-up, with a toy cobbler's bench or workbench, compare a child's version of the tools with the ones you use.

Comment

This is a basic activity to familiarize your child with the care and use of certain tools. It is a way to introduce a younger child to the world of mechanical ideas and the uses of tools and machines.

Evaluation

1. Was your child able to understand the way certain tools are used?
2. Did your child listen to your explanation of the proper use of the tools and attempt to operate them correctly?
3. Did you both get satisfaction from working together and cleaning up the work area?

Older Child—Inventory

Materials: pen and paper; tools; masking tape and permanent ink marker *or* label maker

1. Ask your child to help you inventory your tools.
2. Mention that you have decided to put a label on each tool.
3. Have your child place together all the tools used for particular tasks. This may require some explanation on your part. Together, you can recall the last time certain tools were used.
4. Take turns printing the names of the tools on the tape (or using the label maker and attaching labels to the handles of the tools).
5. Decide with the child where each tool should be placed, and on a sheet of paper, record its name as you put it away.
6. If there are tools that need oiling or sharpening,

demonstrate, and then let your child help you put them in good working order.

7. As a follow-up, ask your child if he or she has a set of tools, or a collection of any kind with which he or she would like some help in labeling and organizing. If so, offer to assist with the task.

Comment

This activity can take place over a period of several days. It helps your child understand that one must know the proper names of tools and have them organized and properly cared for so that they can be found and used when needed. The follow-up activity allows your child to take the lead in carrying out a project with some of his or her own important possessions. You are showing mutual respect and a willingness to learn from each other.

Evaluation

1. Did your child take an active role, or tend to watch? Did there seem to be interest?

2. Did you feel that you not only accomplished something, but also had a good time?

FOR FAMILY TIME

BIRTHDAYS

Younger Child—My Birth Day

Materials: (all optional) paper; pencil, pen, or magic marker

1. Tell the story of the day your child was born, from the father's perspective. If you were not physically present, tell what you were doing when you learned of

the birth. If your child is adopted or you joined the family after his or her birth, tell the story of your first meeting. This is your child's day, so do not dwell on unpleasant incidents, if there were any.

Be prepared for lots of questions and requests for retelling. Everyone likes to be the main character in a story, and your child will probably try to prolong the story as much as possible. There is no need to be overtechnical. Watch your child's reaction to the story.

2. Tell what other members of the family were doing on the day of your child's birth.
3. Gather pictures of your child from the time of your first meeting to his or her present birthday. Provide a childhood picture of yourself to show how your appearance has changed. Emphasize the strong points in your child's personality and physical development. This is not a day for criticsm. Allow your child to suggest some of his or her best characteristics.
4. If your child wishes, let him or her use plain paper and crayon, pencil, or magic markers to draw him- or herself at birth and on this birthday.
5. If pictures are drawn, let your child describe the illustrations.
6. At intervals, ask your child to tell you about the day he or she was born, or when he or she first met you. Such conversations should include a statement from you that you are pleased that he or she is a part of the family.

Comment

One result of this activity may be that the child will begin to reflect on his or her own positive characteristics. Another is that your child will sense the importance to the family of his or her birth. Your child will experience the reality of developmental change from infancy to early childhood and may realize that relationships also can change and grow over time.

Evaluation
1. Do you think your child felt good about him- or herself when hearing about the birth day?
2. Was your child able to suggest some of his or her own positive characteristics?

Older Child—Being Part of a Family

Materials: same as for younger child

1.—6. Same as for younger child.
7. Sometime during your child's birthday, make a point of saying that you are glad he or she was born into your family, or that you were able to become an important person in his or her life. Tell some specific things you would never have done if he or she had not been born. Examples: school involvement, sports activities, family activities at church, visits to parks and zoos, kite-flying, computer games, hugs at night, etc. Tell your child you enjoyed your own childhood activities *and* the opportunity to participate in new activities with him or her.
8. Ask if things would have been different for your child if he or she had been born into another family. If so, how? (Depending on your family circumstances and the child's present mood, there may be some negative comments. This isn't a time for you to criticize.)
9. Discuss the good things about being part of your own family.

Comment
This brief activity is intended to assure your child of a special place in the family or in your life. It also can help you see the uniqueness of your own family and its good attributes.

Evaluation
1. Was your child able to accept your comments about the positive results of coming into the family?
2. Did you each listen to the other?

3. Was your child able to think of good aspects of being part of your family? Why, or why not, do you think?

VALUES I—CHOICES

Younger Child

Materials: food items

Modeling values (demonstrating values by your own words and deeds) is one of the most effective teaching methods. It confirms for your child the importance of a belief, possession, commitment. The following suggestions are meant to assist your child in developing the capacity and experience for making decisions. They are *not* meant to minimize the worth of your own example.

1. Give your child choices, when possible, and abide by his or her decision. Examples:

"Which shall we do first—buy the ice-cream cone, or pick out the get-well card for Grandma?"

"Would you like peas or carrots for dinner tonight?"
"Shall we take a walk around the block, or swing in the backyard?"
"Do you want to wash the wheels, or the chrome?"

2. Occasionally, ask why a particular choice was made. Ask if it was easy or difficult to make the choice.
3. Place several food items on the table. Ask your child to pick up each one and tell why it would or would not be a good choice to eat. (Some items, such as chocolate, which give quick energy but can promote tooth decay, would fall into both categories.) Food suggestions: whole wheat bread and white bread, sweetened and unsweetened cereal, carrot and apple, apple juice and fruit punch, lunchmeat and hamburger, pudding and cookies.
4. Sample some of the choices.

Comment

By being given the opportunity to decide, your child is learning the concept of choices. The importance or interest of each possible choice will help to determine its value and the final selection. This is a building block from which you can begin to deal with moral values and issues when the child is older.

Evaluation

1. Were you able to abide by your child's decisions when he or she was given a choice?
2. Were you able to tell whether your child really thought about the choices, or randomly selected one?

Older Child

Materials: none

1.—2. Same as for younger child. The choices of an older child may be more mature. Examples:
   "Will you choose to play football and basketball at school, or join the Boy Scouts?"
   "Which do you think would be the better donation—

to the Easter Seal campaign or to the Fire-Fighters raffle?"
3. Tell stories from your childhood, make up stories, or use stories from religious or school literature that deal with questions of values. Keep them very short and allow your child to tell you what he or she thinks is a good choice, and why. (Be sure to find out why. Otherwise, your child may tell you only what he or she thinks you want to hear). Examples:
   a. The school rule was no cutting in line. But Ted's friend Mike had twisted his ankle at recess. Ted thought he shouldn't be standing on that foot such a long time. Should he allow Mike to cut in front of him?
   b. Alice often teased Patty's friend Sue. One day Patty saw Sue take a homework paper from Alice's notebook, to get even. Sue made Patty promise not to tell. Because Alice didn't turn in her homework, the teacher gave her a double assignment that night. Should Patty tell the teacher that Sue had taken Alice's paper?
3. Tell your child about choices you make in the course of your daily life. Invite your child to tell about choices he or she has made.

Comment

As children gain experience in making choices, they begin to understand the thinking that goes into making decisions. You can help your child think of the good and bad points of each possible decision. The short stories will help you both struggle with the question of right and wrong in various situations. The struggle may help each of you develop your own set of guidelines for behavior.

Evaluation

1. What did your child's choices tell you about his or her moral development? Did he or she think the punishment should fit the crime, regardless of intent?

2. Were decisions based on desire for your approval?
3. Did your child seem self-centered, or was he or she able to view situations as a member of a larger group?
4. What motives prompt *your* decisions?

VALUES II—SOMEBODY ELSE'S SHOES

Younger Child

Materials: none

1. Visit a hospital-supply store. With permission, allow your child to touch and examine wheelchairs, leg braces, crutches, etc. Explain their uses.
2. Have your child tell you about the equipment, to be sure he or she understands.
3. After leaving the store, tell about someone you know who has used one of those items. Does your child know anyone? Would it be difficult or easy to use the equipment?
4. Talk about yourselves or about others you know who have had some injury or operation. Did the cast (or operation) change those people? Does a cut or a scrape change us?
5. Begin to make a point of telling your child how you feel about various behaviors. Examples:
    "Thank you for taking your plate to the kitchen. I felt relieved that I didn't have to clear the table by myself."
    "When you play that record, I feel like tapping my feet."
    "When you yell at your big brother, I feel like yelling at you."
6. Occasionally, in the middle of an activity, ask the child about his or her feelings. Examples: during cleanup, at end of a TV show, while playing marbles, first thing in the morning, while putting toys away, after a quarrel with a sibling or friend.

Comment

Moral development, the growing awareness of right and wrong, takes place as persons observe those about them, hear the viewpoints of others, and deal with various value-systems at home, at school, with friends, and perhaps in church or synagogue. The task of adults is to demonstrate (1) by example and (2) through support and conversation, both our importance as individuals and our responsibilities as members of larger groups. Share a patriotic, religious, or ethnic/racial heritage, if this is part of your own belief-system. If not, you can explain these and other perspectives as one way of helping your child understand his or her relationship to others.

Evaluation

1. Do you think that you and your child are becoming more aware of your own and other people's feelings?
2. Are you able to see others' behavior from their perspective? Is your child?
3. Is your child able to see others as fellow human beings, without regard to handicap, race, or sex?

Older Child

Materials: none

1.—4. Same as for younger child. With permission, allow your child to use a standard wheelchair and a motorized wheelchair. Let your child work at it until he or she can go forward, backward, and turn around. Ask if it was difficult to learn to operate the chair. Would it take skill to have to go everywhere by wheelchair?
5. Occasionally, in the middle of some activity, tell your child how you feel about yourself or about him or her. Examples:

   "When you leave my wrench on the garage floor, I feel that you think I am not important."

"I become depressed when my boss gives me overtime without asking if it is convenient for me." "When you help your sister with her homework, I feel grateful. I feel like working on a project with you."

6. Ask your child about his or her feelings at various times. Examples: after an argument, when baby-sitting for a younger sibling, after winning a game. Make it a point to ask how he or she thinks the other participant felt.
7. Read or tell about newspaper articles, or watch the evening news on TV. Take turns telling how you think people *felt* in certain situations and *why* they behaved in a particular way. (It is not important that you agree with another's behavior or thoughts. The idea here is to gain skill in understanding the reasons behind certain behaviors.) Do not limit yourself to conflict situations. The editorial, sports, and feature sections also provide interesting subjects and situations.

Comment
Same as for younger child.

Evaluation
Same as for younger child.

OUTINGS I—NATURE

Younger Child—"Nature Animals"

Materials: clothesline (plastic or fiber)

Many families enjoy evening strolls, camping trips, walks through the park, trips to the zoo, and so on, as ways to enjoy nature. You can get a glimpse of nature in your own backyard or apartment common space, with this game.
1. With the clothesline, make a big circle on the ground.
2. All family members get into the circle on hands and knees. You will all be "nature animals," exploring.

3. Each chooses an animal to be. Then look, listen, smell, and feel as many things as you can, inside the circle.
4. After 60 seconds, sit down and take turns telling about something you experienced as a "nature animal." Each person may have more than one turn. If a "nature animal" wishes, let him or her show the rest of you a discovery.

Comment

The setting does not need to be an exotic wonderland for family members to enjoy the feel of dirt, prickles of grass and weeds, and sharp points of pebbles. And with everyone on hands and knees, each has approximately the same perspective.

Evaluation
1. Did all members of the family attend to what the others described?
2. Did you notice enthusiasm and a sense of discovery in yourself and in the others?
3. What type of animals did your child act out? How did you feel when you made the sound of an animal?

Older Child—People in Nature

Materials: nursery (greenhouse); setting in nature (optional); landscaping books, house-and-garden magazines, animal habitat books (optional)

Your family may enjoy nature in city parks, on sightseeing trips, through camping, or by some other means. In any of these settings, it is possible to observe humankind's effect on the environment. Adapt the activity to the particular setting you frequent with your family.
1. Explain that you are going to visit a nursery to find out how people work with plants.
2. As a family, visit a local nursery.
3. As individuals (or as teams if there are preschoolers in your family) decide whether you will be gathering

information on: (a) shrubs and trees, (b) flowers and plants, or (c) dirt, chemicals, and implements.

4. Everyone may explore the whole nursery, but each person should pay particular attention to his or her particular assignment.

5. After an allotted time, meet near the check-out counter (or some other spot). If there is something new or unusual that anyone wants to show the others, take time to look.

6. After you leave the greenhouse, allow each individual or team to tell about what was seen and learned.

7. When you are home, look at your own yard, apartment complex, or street, and decide together how people have used nature there.

8. Let each person tell what responsibility he or she should have in caring for nature (or "God's world," if that expression is used in your home). Decide if your family could make any improvements at your home setting.

9. As a follow-up, repeat steps 7 and 8 when you visit formal city gardens, the neighborhood park, a national park.
10. As another follow-up, use books and magazines that show the natural habitat of certain plants and animals to discover how nature provides for itself.
11. House-and-garden magazines may give you some ideas for using human skills to improve upon nature around your own home.

Comment

This activity is intended to help your family see the partnership of people and nature. The trip to the nursery can be an education in the prevention of plant disease and in the human ingenuity involved in developing new strains of plants.

Evaluation

1. How would you rate the sharing time you had after leaving the nursery?
2. Is your family developing a sense of responsibility for the natural world?

OUTINGS II—CULTURE

Younger Child—Program, Anyone?

Materials: programs from a cultural event; props used at such an event (optional)

1. After you have told your family that all of you will be attending a concert or exhibition, invite them to attend an imaginary event with you.
2. Act as an usher—pass out programs and escort family members to their seats (or act as a museum guide if it is an art exhibition).
3. Act as master of ceremonies (or guide) as you refer to each of the items on the program. Use any props you have that would normally be used at such an event. Examples: stick for conductor's baton, musical

instrument, artist's (or house painter's) paintbrush, period clothing for an opera or play. Include humor as well as serious moments (it's all right for a child to giggle while watching dad play an imaginary violin).

4. Invite family members to take impromptu parts in the "performance."
5. When you actually attend the performance, be sure that each family member receives a program; refer to it before show time and during intermission. Take time to go backstage, if at all possible.
6. Collect all the programs from the family members after the performance.
7. Sometime after this event, use the programs and repeat steps 1—4 with your family. During this imaginary performance, family members may switch roles.

Comment

This activity allows the family group to "get into" some cultural events. It is a way to understand the process of the event, and the feelings of those who present such events. It also provides family play-acting fun.

Evaluation

1. Were the imaginary cultural events fun?
2. Did the family members enter into the "pretend" situations spontaneously?
3. Do you feel that this kind of activity brings your family closer together?
4. Is your child beginning to appreciate his or her own artistic talents and those of others?

Older Child—Prelude

Materials: place of concert or display; encyclopedias or records (optional)

1. If possible, visit the building where a concert, play, or display which your family plans to attend will take place. Look for special features that will assist in the

event. Examples: lighting in a museum, set for a play, seating in a concert hall (or high school auditorium).

2. If possible, make your visit during a rehearsal or when a display is being arranged. Watch a bit of the practice (or arranging).
3. Depending on the event you will attend, listen to one of the pieces on a record, find samples of the kind of art you will see and find out what technique was used, get the script and look at the stage directions, visit a music store and examine the instruments that will be used.
4. Attend the cultural event as a family.
5. As a follow-up, take turns finding comparisons between the practice and the actual event. Compare your feelings about being in the building before with your feelings during the performance. Give each person a chance to tell a difference or similarity.
6. As another follow-up, make a list of things that were necessary for the performance. Examples: talented people, practice, builders to construct the building, instruments (including brush and palate, sheet music), organizers of the event, spectators.
7. For another follow-up, see steps 1—4 for younger child.

Comment

It is easy to be an uninformed spectator at cultural (or sport) events. In this activity, you are acknowledging the effort and talent necessary to produce a cultural event for the public. We all gain more respect for an art when we understand it better. Family members, no matter what their age, can learn from one another during this activity.

Evaluation

1. Is there growing respect for the fine arts among the family members?
2. Were they willing to learn from one another?
3. Did anyone exclude him- or herself from the activity? Why, or why not?

FAMILY HISTORY

Younger Child—Interviewing Family Members

Materials: notebook; notebook paper; pen or pencil; crayon or magic markers (optional); tape recorder

1. Prepare an Interview Sheet. Example:

INTERVIEW SHEET

Person Interviewed:

Address:

School (or) Place of Work:

Interviewer:

Questions: 1.
              2. Etc. . . .

2. Make enough copies for all the family members, and a couple of extras. Duplicating machines can be found at post offices, libraries, and banks, as well as at many places of business, or copies can be typed or handwritten.

3. At a time when the family members are together, interview the youngest speaking member of the family with a tape recorder, by paraphrasing the following:

Hello. I'm Kermit the Frog. Today I'm interviewing (child's name), who lives in the (family name) home at (address). (Child's name) attends the (school). Now, (child's name),

1. Which foods do you like most?
2. What are your favorite activities?
3. Who is your best friend?
4. What was the best time in your life?
5. What was the worst time in your life?
6. What famous person do you like most?
7. Which are your favorite television characters:
8. What job would you like when you grow up?
9. What is your favorite story (or book)?
10. What do you think life will be like in the future?

4. Interview all family members, using these questions or making up others. Allow each person a chance to interview and to be interviewed.

5. Taking turns, over a period of a couple of days (a week for a large family), allow interviewers to listen to their tapes and transfer the answers to the Interview Sheets. Children who do not yet write can dictate to an older sibling or parent.

6. As the Interview Sheets are completed, they can be inserted in the notebook.

7. As an optional activity, add a couple of illustrations on the Interview Sheets, or on separate pieces of paper, with an explanatory note at the bottom of the page.

8. As a group, make up a title for the family book.

9. As a follow-up, take turns telling something you each learned about another family member from listening to and reading the interviews.

Comment

This activity illustrates for all family members that each has opinions, feelings, and interests, and that these can be similar or different. This collection of profiles can serve to introduce friends to the family members and to the life-style of the family.

Evaluation
1. Who answered with fantasy-level responses? with realism? enthusiastically? with embarrassment?
2. Who enjoyed interviewing? being interviewed? How well did interviewers listen to the person they were interviewing?
3. Have you looked through the profiles individually or as a group?

Older Child—Family Album/Interview

Materials: notebook; notebook paper; tape recorder; family albums; paper and pencil

1—9. Same as for younger child.
10. Sit with your child and look through family picture albums. Point out family members and friends, both living and dead. Share incidents about them.
11. Ask your child, "What do you think life was like back when (friend or relative) was a (boy or girl) your age?"
12. Help your child construct questions around the following areas: social, emotional, cognitive, physical, spiritual. Examples:
    Did men and women have the same jobs?
    What games did boys and girls play?
    What did people do before television?
    What did they do when they were angry?
    Were people more religious?

What was it like before computers, or before telephones?

13. Encourage your child to interview an older person, either family or non-family. Use these questions and/or others. Record the interview.

14. Prepare an Interview Sheet (see step 1 for younger child).

15. Listen to the recorded interview together and help your child transfer the answers to the Interview Sheet.

16. Depending on the person interviewed, select an appropriate title for each interview, such as "City Slicker Grows Up."

17. Ask your child what he or she learned from this experience.

18. As a follow-up, begin a weekly diary, and invite your child to do so. You may each decide whether your own diary will be private or will be shared.

Comment

Many people lose the connection with their family roots. It is important for significant adults to help spark and cultivate a child's interest in family background. This focus on mature adults, friend and family, may also help children feel an increased respect for their elders.

Evaluation

1. Was your child comfortable in interviewing an adult?
2. Was he or she able to independently interview the friend or family member? How much did you help?
3. Did you or your child ever refer to the Interview Sheet at a later time?
4. Is your child developing a respect for his or her elders?

MEALTIMES

Younger Child and Older Child—Centerpieces

Materials: craft supplies for the project you select

1. Choose a simple centerpiece project from a craft book (or use your imagination) to represent the current season. Example: Tree branch with glued-on crushed tissue-paper "buds," to represent spring. Container could be coffee can filled with pebbles and covered with aluminum foil.
2. During a meal when all family members are present, explain that you would like to brighten the table with a seasonal centerpiece, and you would like everyone's help.
3. Assign each person a task. Example: find a branch about 12-18″ long; cover the coffee can with aluminum foil; and so on.
4. At a time you select, perhaps before or after a family meal, assemble the completed assignments and combine them into the finished product.
5. Display the centerpiece on the table for the duration of the season.
6. As the next season approaches, ask for two volunteers to plan a new centerpiece. The team should include one person who can read.
7. Allow the team leaders to repeat steps 3—5 with the family.
8. Repeat the procedure for each season. The family members may wish to arrange special centerpieces for certain religious holidays, birthdays, or other special occasions.
9. As a follow-up, plan an occasional meal around a certain theme or country and allow each family member to assist in the preparations.

Comment

This activity allows family members to focus on making the table (and mealtimes) more pleasant. A by-product is the cooperation involved in completing the centerpiece.

Evaluation

1. Was there enthusiasm?

2. How well did family members cooperate?
3. Was the project referred to in later conversations?

TRIPS

Younger Child—Planning a Trip

Materials: construction paper; magic marker; accordion file; maps; brochures

1. Using ads in magazines, places family members have heard about, and features in the newspaper, pick out several places where the family would like to go. Include ideas for afternoon excursions and day trips, as well as vacation ideas. Choose only places you could actually visit. (For instance, if a trip to Disneyland would take too long or cost too much, the adult can have "veto power" on that idea.)
2. Write letters asking for information (call if in the same town), or fill out coupons. Use your *child's* name in the return address.
3. As the information arrives, look it over together and then have your child file each location in a separate section of the accordion file. Label the file for easy reference.
4. If you belong to an automobile club, secure a map of each state and city in which you are interested. Or write to the chamber of commerce in each city and the highway department of each state. (Your local chamber of commerce can give you addresses.)
5. When you have received most of the information, make 3 signs with construction paper and a magic marker. The signs will say, In Town, Day Trip, and Vacation.
6. Separate your information into the three categories.
7. On separate occasions, look at the material from each category and make a choice together. You might decide through conversation alone, or you could take a

vote. If it is your habit to vote on family matters, make sure no one person always loses. Appreciating (or tolerating) others' interests is part of family life.

It might be wise to make one of the In Town visits first, so that there is reinforcement for making decisions in the other two areas.

8. As you visit the sites, pick up additional brochures and other items to add to your file. These will serve as reminders when you are remembering the trip.

Comment

One purpose of this activity is to show the family members how decisions are made. Your child will experience the way group members listen and are listened to, agree and disagree, and come to a decision.

Evaluation

1. What was each person's degree of involvement? Was each member happy with the decision?
2. Did the group members enjoy (or dislike) the trip as they had thought they would?

Older Child—Planning a Trip

Materials: same as for younger child

1—8. Same as for younger child.
9. Break down job tasks for implementing the trip: travel time, costs, packing and transportation of baggage, length of stay.
10. Older children might enjoy visiting the local library to research the historical importance of sites.

Comment

It is always interesting to note the role a child plays in group discussions. The level of activity illustrates your child's style of group behavior in other situations—in school or with peers.

Evaluation

Same as for younger child.

FAMILY CONFLICT AND RESOLUTION

Younger Child—The Difference Game

Materials: large pieces of paper; crayons or colored markers

Family members frequently come into conflict about many types of issues. It is important for a younger child to recognize and become comfortable with the subtle and not so subtle differences in behavior, attitude, and personality of family members. Acceptance of these differences allows a small child the opportunity to begin to come to grips with conflict situations. This activity can be carried out with your child alone, or it can be shared with others in the family.

1. Talk with your child about his or her perceptions of family members (their behavior, attitudes, personality), and don't forget to include yourself.
2. In your discussion, explain that behaviors are things people do (hugging someone); that attitudes are ideas, which are part of the way people think (disliking the next-door neighbors); and that personality consists of the emotions that people have (happiness, anger, fear, sadness).
3. Using sheets of newsprint or wrapping paper, write the name of each person in the household at the top of a separate sheet. On each sheet, make 3 columns: one headed Behavior, a second Attitudes, and a third Personality. Or you may draw picture symbols for those words.
4. Ask your child to name some different characteristics of people in the household. If your child is very young, you may want to give suggestions. Example: "Your sister Sherry likes to play softball." In the beginning, young children may imitate the responses of others.

This should not be discouraged; with practice your child will begin to initiate his or her own responses.

5. Ask your child to attempt to identify at least one characteristic in each category (note that younger children will identify behaviors more readily than other characteristics). With practice, your child's perceptions will develop.
6. Discuss the similarities and differences in family members' perceptions of one another in a nonjudgmental manner.
7. Once you have practiced this activity, ask your child to identify things about others that may cause a problem or conflict.
8. The family group could then brainstorm to find solutions to such a conflict.
9. Ask the person who is the source of the problem to choose those solutions with which he or she will attempt to deal with the problem.
10. If the conflict continues, bring up suggestions at a family meeting as to how the situation might be further handled.

Comment

In building a person's ability to solve problems within human relationships, knowledge and awareness of others is essential. We all need to become sensitized to the ways we are different and, at the same time, alike. If family members can identify and then discuss these characteristics, their acceptance of one another may be enhanced. Each person is important in his or her own right. This activity lends itself to consideration of both positive and negative characteristics.

Evaluation

1. Was it easy, or difficult, for your child to identify behaviors, attitudes, or personality characteristics?
2. Were you able to gain a better sense of the way your child perceives the family unit?
3. Do you think this activity will assist your child and yourself in coping with conflict situations?

Older Child—Problem Solving/Conflict Resolution

Materials: paper and pencil

1. At a family meeting, ask your to child identify a problem or conflict which he or she thinks is troubling the family unit.
2. Write out problems, or draw pictures to help visually portray the problem identified.
3. Each person should have an opportunity to give his or her ideas and an explanation as to what may be causing the difficulty. Since older children are capable of thinking on a more sophisticated level, they can see family events more clearly and should be able to list causes.
4. After problems and proposed causes have been identified, ask your child for possible solutions. List all possible solutions offered, no matter how illogical they may sound.
5. After your child has offered suggestions, add your own to the list.
6. Now discuss the practicality of the solutions. Remember to try to respond honestly to your own, as well as to your child's suggestions. Be careful not to diminish your child's willingness to offer a solution by discounting his or her response.
7. Try to decide on at least one possible solution to the problem. After the suggestion has been tried, reevaluate its effect at a later time.

Comment

This activity assumes a high level of interaction between you, your child, and any other family member involved in the conflict situation. As your child gives feedback, he or she may become more interested in resolving the problem situation.

Evaluation

1. To what degree was your child able to identify and discuss the nature of the conflict?

2. How did you feel as you shared your ideas with your child?
3. Do you think the solutions being discussed had merit?
4. How did this process help solve problems between you, your child, and other family members?
5. What learning occurred for any younger child who listened to the interaction between the older child and adults?

FOR LIFE CRISES

NEW BABY

Younger Child—Our Baby

Materials: magazines; pictures of child as a baby; baby doll; equipment for new baby

Crises are not necessarily negative. Occasionally they may bring pleasure, and almost always, they provide potential for personal growth. For a younger child, the arrival of a new baby in the home can be both an exciting and an overwhelming experience. A young child is at times confused by the changes that are taking place. Your involvement with your child in the issue of new birth can be critical in showing him or her how men can respond to the nurturing process. It is also a way you can show your child that he or she will continue to be someone special. Remember, much of what you do will depend on the age and stage of development of your child.

1. Tell your child that a new baby will be coming to live in your house. It is growing in a special pocket, a uterus, inside mommy's body.

2. You and your child can feel the baby kicking. Ask the mother to tell you when the baby is moving, so that you are all aware that the baby is growing big and strong enough to be born and live with you outside mommy's body.
3. Learn about the characteristics of babies. Examples: Look at pictures of new babies in magazines; visit a friend or neighbor who has a new baby, or visit a church nursery; compare newborn puppies or kittens to adult dogs and cats; look at earlier pictures of your child and compare to him or her at present.
4. Purchase (if you don't already have one) a natural looking (and feeling) baby doll. This may be your child's "baby."
5. Play-act, with your child's doll, the new baby's arrival.
6. Allow your child to repeat the play-acting, taking your part and then the mother's part, or to make up other situations.

7. At bedtime, at story time, or at some other talking time during the day, tell your child some of the needs the baby will have—eating, changing, bathing, sleeping. Ask your child for suggestions about how to meet those needs, and then offer some information yourself. Example: Bathing. Your child may suggest giving the baby a bath in the bathtub. Your comment might be that the baby *will* use warm water and a special soap and that a bathtub is a good place for getting clean. But because the baby will be so small, it will need a special small bathtub. Show the tub, soap, baby washcloths and towels (if you use them).

8. Decide together what each of you can do to help with the baby. For instance, you could put the warm water into the tub and carry it to the table; your child could get the baby's cloth and towel; and the mother could undress the baby.

9. As a follow-up, you could practice some of these routines with the child's doll. Be sure to explain that each baby is different, and so some things might need to be changed when the baby actually comes home.

Comment

This type of activity allows a child an opportunity to "preview" what is going to happen prior to its actual occurrence. By acting out a number of possible situations, your child becomes more aware of his or her own part in this event, as well as your role. Gradually, your child learns how to relate to this new person without feeling displaced.

Evaluation

1. How did you feel while you were explaining your role in regard to the new arrival?

2. How did you respond to your child during the role-plays? Were you at ease in discussing and acting out what was to happen?

3. Did your child enjoy being involved in the role-play? What kind of questions did your child ask about his or her, and about your, relationship to the new baby?

Older Child—New Responsibilities

Materials: reference book; equipment for new baby

1. Let your older child be among the first to know that a new baby will be added to the family. When you tell him or her, be sure to stress that because of your love for your partner and hers for you, you decided to become a family. You then wanted to share this love with a child (or children), and you still have enough love to share with the baby who is developing.
2. Review with your child the way a baby is conceived and develops before birth. Go to the library or a good reference source to help you discuss the basic ideas about conception and development of the fetus.
3. Before the baby arrives, talk about the name of the baby, where the baby will sleep, what kind of furniture will be in the baby's room (or part of the room), and how your older child can help with the baby. These are all ways to help him or her feel that the new baby will be a family affair.
4. As a follow-up, allow your child the opportunity to assist in the preparation for the new arrival: readying the room, helping to buy diapers and other basic items. If you purchase school supplies or clothes, or car-pool to after-school club meetings or lessons, mention that this is a way you care for your older child.
5. Talk about the changes that will take place when the new baby arrives. How will people need to act toward the baby? What will each person's responsibilities be? Will routines be altered?
6. Decide on the kinds of tasks the older child can assume with the new baby: walking the baby, holding the baby when he or she needs to be burped, giving the bottle, and so on. Also decide how each family member will help the others, for the new baby will not be the only important person in the family.

Comment

Older children are more able to be active participants in such an event. The more involved your child is, the easier the transition will be for everyone.

Evaluation

1. How did your child feel about these new responsibilities?
2. Was he or she able to participate in decisions regarding the new baby?

SEPARATION/DIVORCE

Younger Child—Love and Disagreements

Materials: none

Separation and divorce are difficult for a child of five or younger to understand. They are often painful for an adult to explain to a child. Even so, it is important to give your child the opportunity to work through some basic ideas related to preparation for divorce.

1. As simply as you can, tell your child that you and the mother will not be living together for a while (or ever again, in the case of divorce). Tell your child that both of you will continue to love him or her, even though you will not all be living together.
2. Ask your child where an aunt, a cousin, a grandmother, or another relative lives. Ask your child if grandma (aunt, etc.) loves him or her, even though grandma and your child do not live together. After several examples, explain that you (or the mother) also will keep on loving. Repeat this conversation occasionally until you are satisfied that your child understands and believes it. (During the first visits, or upon returning home if you have custody, use good times to reinforce this idea.)
3. When you see older siblings or neighbors arguing, remark that you wish it were not happening. Say that

you wish you could stop the argument, even though it is not your fault. At another time when a quarrel is observed, ask if the disagreement is your child's fault. Assuming that it is not, ask if he or she wishes it would stop. Ask how it feels when the quarrel does not stop.

4. If convenient, take your child aside right then and compare the ongoing quarrel to the dissolution of his or her parents' relationship. Tell your child very directly that it is not his or her fault and that your child cannot stop the event, no matter how much he or she might want to. Then let your child tell you how he or she feels. Do not pass judgment on those feelings.

5. After your child has been in a fuss with a playmate, ask how he or she feels about the playmate, and about the fuss. Say that if two people have big disagreements, or if they continually have little disagreements, they cannot be happy together. Add that this is one of the reasons you and your partner are separating.

6. If it is actually the case, point out that it is easier for you and your partner to be friends when you are not together so much. (Do *not* say this to your child if it is not so.) Also, point out that it is easier for you to have a good time with your child when you are not always disagreeing with your partner. The divorce can be a way for your child to enjoy both you and your ex-partner in your separate lives and interests.

7. List with your child the kinds of activities in which he or she can take part while spending time with each parent.

8. Pretend to be one of your child's playmates. Ask why his or her parents do not live together anymore. Let the child respond. Talk about this together until you both are satisfied with a brief answer that your child can share with others.

Comment

It is important to free your child from feeling responsible for the inability of his or her parents to resolve their differences. Drawing a comparison with other arguments and with the child's own conflicts with siblings or friends may help to clarify the difficulties the parents are having.

Evaluation
1. How did you feel about the explanation you were able to give?
2. What do you feel your child was able to comprehend? Did he or she ask questions or offer comments?
3. What activities are of interest to both you and your child?

Older Child—Reasons

Materials: none

With age comes the ability to reason more capably. In many instances an older child is affected more severely, since he or she has developed stronger emotional bonds, and also may have been caught up in the conflict-ridden relationship of the parents.

1. If you think your child is able to understand and needs to know, you might discuss the separation or divorce in some detail. Do not suggest that your child choose sides. If you are very angry, hurt, or guilty, your child will probably have picked up the feeling anyway, so you can be open about telling the reasons without dwelling on them. This may clear the air and help your child understand how he or she fits into the new situation without an abundance of fear, desire for retaliation, or feelings of rejection or anxiety.
2. Same as steps 1—7 for younger child.

Comment
Same as for younger child.

Evaluation
1. Did your child feel comfortable, or uncomfortable, when asked to discuss the circumstances of the separation or divorce?

2. Did you feel that your child understood the rationale for what was happening to him or her and between you and your partner?

DEATH

Younger Child—What Is Death?

Materials: photo album

The separation and loss a child may feel after the death of someone close will vary, depending on the individual. Regardless of the intensity, death needs to be explained as a part of our everyday existence, something we should expect to happen. With younger children, the fact that the deceased is no longer a part of the everyday environment is confusing and warrants clarification. A child also needs an opportunity to experience grief, or a mourning process. The first 3 ideas below will introduce the idea of death *before* the loss of a relative, friend, or pet occurs.

1. When the two of you see a dead animal or bug, take time to look at it. Ask if it moves. Has it begun to decay? (Dead plants and animals slowly become earth again.) Note other characteristics of lifelessness— stiffness, color change, shriveled appearance.
2. Introduce your child to some of the death rituals by placing a dead bug in a tissue or in a small box and burying it, placing a marker at the grave. (The child can do the digging and select the marker.) Say that in this way, we show respect for one of God's creatures. Point out that the remains of the animal are like a covering, or shell, that once housed the living, feeling part of the animal.
3. Go to a cemetery occasionally. Look for names and ages on the markers; note the veterans' flags and the flowers from recent burials. Explain that people are buried to show respect for them.

4. When a loved one dies, explain very clearly that the person's body is dead and will never be alive again. But for us, the person's spirit, the thinking and feeling part of the person, will live forever. We will remember and continue to love the person; the dead person's love for us will also continue. Depending on your religious orientation, you might add that God's love, too, surrounds us during our lifetime, and continues forever.
5. If at all possible, allow your child to see the deceased at a private time. Cry together, ask and answer questions, touch the reality of a dead body.
6. If the deceased is being buried at a cemetery, have your child either attend the burial or vist the cemetery afterward. This will help satisfy the question, "Where does the body go?"
7. Talking about past events in which the deceased and your child have taken part is a way of remembering the good times spent together. A photo album will help your child connect the person and the happenings of the past.

Comment

Although there is a grieving process that a young child may experience, the basic focus of this activity is to express the idea that death is an inevitable part of our life cycle. This activity should give your child an opportunity to begin to understand some of the realities of death.

Evaluation
1. How did your child respond to your explanation of death (ask questions, withdraw, become rowdy)?
2. Did you observe your child grieving for the deceased person during the activity? What behaviors did he or she exhibit?
3. How did you feel about this activity? Did it allow you and your child time to share your thoughts? Were you able to show your feelings, or did you find yourself keeping a "stiff upper lip" before your child?

Older Child—A Life Review

Materials: paper and pencil *or* tape recorder

As a child becomes capable of thinking more logically, he or she begins to see the life/death continuum in a different perspective. The dying process now is more understandable and personalized. Loss and separation take on a meaning your child can focus upon and deal with openly in a more sophisticated manner.

1—7. Same as for younger child.

8. Depending upon your child's association with the deceased, he or she may wish to talk about his or her perceptions, or develop a "portrait" of this person. This can be talked through or drawn.

9. Suggest that you and your child review the special events in which your child and the person who has died were involved.

10. Events can be reviewed through discussion and/or by using pictures or artifacts with which the deceased was associated—something the deceased made or gave the child, snapshots of your child relating to the deceased, and such things.

11. Begin to develop a "collage," or a history, of the person by piecing together particular events that occurred between the child and the deceased, including the impressions and feelings your child has about that person.

12. Depending on your child's creativity, suggest that he or she make a notebook of things that happened with the deceased. The notebook can be as complex as your child wants to make it. It can be filled with pictures drawn by your child, snapshots, writings, or even a recording your child has made relating his or her feelings and ideas about the person. A shoe box or other box can be used to store bulky items.

Comment

This activity serves as a life review for your child as he or she highlights the memories that made up the relationship with the deceased. This activity may allow for a meaningful interchange between you and your child.

Evaluation

1. Did your child show interest in this activity? Why, or why not, do you think?
2. Were you and your child able to share your thoughts about the deceased person? your feelings about dying? about issues of living?
3. Did you participate in this activity with your child? Whose decision was it?

DIMENSIONS OF DEVELOPMENT

INTRODUCTION

The chapter "Your Child" briefly described the five dimensions of developmental growth: social, emotional, cognitive, physical, and spiritual. The activities in Section Two made use of those dimensions in carrying out the activities and in reflecting on the attitudes, feelings, and skills through the Comment and Evaluation ideas. Through these, you can become more aware of your child's physical capacities, spiritual ideas, ability to relate to others personally and in a group, and other characteristics.

Some men and children may be interested in exploring one or more of these dimensions directly. If so, the ideas in this section may be of help. Suggestions will be made for each dimension. You and your child can carry out the given suggestions, or use them to think of others. Since children, even of the same age, have such a wide range of developmental progress, the suggestions are general. You should feel free to experiment until you "find" your child's level, and then advance from there. Do not be surprised to find yourself and your child grappling with some of the same issues in certain areas. Development does not necessarily progress with age. Keep in mind that it is as important to understand and accept a child's stage within a certain dimension of development as it is to help him or her progress to a more advanced level.

SUGGESTIONS FOR THE SOCIAL DIMENSION

THE NATURE OF RELATIONSHIPS

Each of us is involved in a myriad of social relationships. One can be a father, a friend, a brother, a cousin, or a neighbor. Children observe the various roles and begin to understand the demands, joys, and responsibilities of adult life. A man is a feeling and thinking person. This balanced picture of a man as a broadly based person is an emerging one for many. As child and man learn to accept this new image of manhood, both will benefit by learning to live as whole people.

★ Talk about relationships. Share with your child the ups and downs experienced in relationships with others. Tell about your adventures as a boy.

★ Watch television and discuss the relationship of the characters. Do those relationships realistically portray men and women? boys and girls?

★ Discuss the relationships among family members. Think of those relatives in the household and those living outside. Do they all get along well together? How often are they together—playing, visiting, communicating?

★ Draw pictures to exemplify social relationships. Examples: family picnic, persons at work or school, grocery shopping.

★ Think about your child's perception of social events. Does he or she understand, in an appropriate way, the relationship of men and women, siblings, peers, neighbors, and others?

★ Analyze the amount and quality of time you spend with your child. Are you relating to your child in a way that will help him or her understand the dynamics of relationships?

★ People have different roles in various relationships. Together, think of "matching roles"—salesperson/buyer, student/teacher, parent/child, child/adult. Give your child a set of matching roles and have him or her tell you the kinds of behavior appropriate for each subject. Ask your child to give *you* some roles to describe.

INTERACTION

★ Discuss the social relationship you hold with your child. Are you in a biological relationship? Are you becoming integrated into the child's world? Will this relationship be a short-term or a long-term one? Are each of you aware of the potential hurt/satisfaction present in all relationships? Please remember that the closeness being built in your interaction with a child may be one-sided (on the child's part, or on yours). Be considerate and compassionate.

★ Be real and honest with your child. Attempt to enjoy the activity in which you are engaged. Get into contact with your child beyond the task at hand. For example, sweeping the garage is sweeping the garage. But the task takes on an added dimension as you enjoy the time together; as he or she asks questions, helps you, or learns about the world.

★ Spending time together brings you closer to your child. Over time, you will begin to feel comfortable with your child and his or her style of living (especially if you do not live in the same household).

★ Make up stories in which some characters are the leaders, some the followers—"good guys," caring people, selfish people. Give the characters names. Following the story, ask what kind of person so-and-so was. (You might describe one of the characters yourself the first few times you do this activity.)

★ Following an interaction with one person, or with several, tell your child what kind of role you think you played (made people angry, were a good helper, did not participate in the discussion, etc.). Share how you felt in that group. Ask your child to give his or her point of view about the role you played.

★ Occasionally (when you have observed, or the child has described, an incident), ask your child what role he or she played. Compliment examples of being a good group member. Encourage your child to share the way he or she feels in various social situations.

THE CONCEPT OF FAMILY

★ Conscious interaction with family members can build a closeness. However, it takes consistent work to create quality relationships. Remember, a history of poor communication patterns cannot be quickly changed. Select one problem area, and begin to work on that.

★ Spend time together as a group. A group can be a family either by marriage or by conscious identification. With the pervasiveness of divorce, a man may have a meaningful relationship with either his own child or someone else's child. As a man, you should be aware of your role and potential impact on someone else's child. Are you building such bridges between you and your child that you block the road for the biological father? Can you replace the natural parent?

★ Sensitize your child to the varying family constellations found in today's world. Talk about the children in your child's world. Speak in nonjudgmental terms of other families. Attempt to explain family problems: divorce, separation, drinking. Seek the assistance of clergy, library books, and teachers to communicate these lessons of life in an appropriate way.

★ Build up the concept of a family by creating a history. Write letters or journals to future relatives who will need to understand contemporary life. Role-playing would be a useful way to relate the impact of these actions.

★ Watch television and critique the relationships of the characters. Do the actors treat one another with respect? love? How do those relationships differ from those in your own family?

★ Consider and teach the values you wish to share. Values are more effectively modeled by action than by word. Don't say "Do as I say, not as I do." This is a mistake. Your child will imitate the behavior patterns he or she observes you and other adults and peers following.

★ On trips into the community, point out the various families you see. Be respectful of a child's conflict concerning his own family situation. For example, does your child understand the nature of his or her "family" after a divorce? death? remarriage? Let your child express those feelings—they are natural. After a time, a new state of mind will evolve, and your child will merge into the group.

RELATIONSHIP TO COMMUNITY, NATION, AND WORLD

★ Discuss your relationship to people in the community: neighbors, friends, community service personnel. Discuss your child's relationship to those people. Does your child know how to deal with strangers? What happens if one is lost?

★ What jobs does your child understand? Is he or she interested in considering those careers as personal occupations? Can you provide more information on those careers?

★ Screen your child's television viewing habits. What is his or her concept of community, nation, world? How would your child benefit from sharing insights into these concepts?

★ Discuss the way people behave at school, in shopping malls, at movies, in other public places, and in their own homes. What values does your child seem to have concerning proper behavior in various settings?

★ Explore the interrelatedness of all people in the Family of God. Involvement in religious activities can help build a wealth of positive experiences and feelings toward all people. Check the library for books designed to influence your child's positive concept of people in other cultures.

★ Discuss the way people help one another to ensure mutual

survival. For example, what happens if a disaster occurs? Who helps? Point out that government programs are run by people. Emphasize that people are helping people. Discuss such groups that you may be involved in, or religious charities, or assistance from members of one's own family.

SUGGESTIONS FOR THE EMOTIONAL DIMENSION

THE NATURE OF FEELINGS

Each of us experiences a wide range of emotions. Our feelings for a particular person can and do change over time. Feelings also have a wide range of intensity. For example, a child can be very angry because a sibling took a ball, but later, that strong feeling will have lessened.

★ Talk about your feelings. Share with your child your feelings about your job, your partner, your friends, and your child. Emphasize the feeling of love. Say that you love each of the people you have discussed in a different way (if, in fact, you do). Share examples of your anger with those people; then tell how you worked out the misunderstandings.

★ Listen while your child expresses negative feelings. Fighting, verbal or physical, does occur in all homes and among most peer groups. You should attempt to help your child express his or her negative feelings in words, rather than through physical force. It may be useful to say, "The better choice is to use words, not fists, when you are angry." Setting an appropriate example while expressing negative emotions is most important. It is also important to transcend the traditional model of "man as aggressor."

★ Assess the degree to which you are attuned to your own

emotions. Men have been traditionally brought up to be unemotional and rational. They often block their feelings. Is it sufficient to share your emotion only with a woman? We, the authors, believe not. Perhaps a critical review of your emotional relationships with other men, your father and mother, children, and women is in order. Men's support groups can offer much assistance in this area.

★ Make up situations, read stories, or watch TV shows. Does your child understand the emotions of the characters involved? Do you and your child think the emotions displayed were appropriate to the situations? Talk about times when it is all right to be angry, jealous, sad, happy, disgusted, bored. What are some good ways to handle those particular feelings?

★ Is your child inhibited in expressing emotion? To what degree does your child let out emotion? Does your child tend to hold in, or to let out, his or her feelings? Why?

★ Does your child, or do you, let out stored up feelings when expressing positive and/or negative feelings? Many of us carry feelings around for years, until later we dump them onto others. It is important to deal with each incident and relationship on its own merit.

★ Emotions can be explored in family meetings where members communicate their opinions, perspectives, and emotions about real issues. For example, group consideration of matters affecting the group may be in order. Final decision and responsibility may lie with the adults, but each member can be involved in providing input. Examples: Should we take a vacation in the mountains or at the beach? Which movie or television program shall we watch? What food shall we serve at a cookout, and how will each member help with the preparations? How do we feel when our ideas are accepted? rejected?

TEACHING ABOUT LOVE

Your child should understand that there are different types of love. You might focus on one type in teaching your child about love—love within the context of the family. In contemporary society, a man can help build a child's concept of family even though he does not live with the child or is not married to the child's mother. Example: an adult male companion (society's common label of boyfriend is seen as a lesser status and is often a misnomer for many adult man-woman relationships). Love in a family includes the feeling between parents, siblings, and extended family members.

★ Love is a different feeling in our relationships with friends, pets, favorite foods or vacation spots. There is also *agape* love, the love that is extended to humankind in general and to all of creation. Some forms of love may seem to be innate (like the "love" of a baby toward the ones who care for him or her), or they may begin as an unexplained chemical reaction toward another person. Other forms of love can be learned as we grow toward responsible adulthood.

★ Share your feelings concerning women. Specify a comprehensive view of women—people with jobs, feelings, skills, the ability to function with or without men, and with or without children. The same views should be offered concerning men. Examples of contemporary forms of roles: women as career people without children, single men as nurturers of children, fathers as thinking and feeling people, women as both wage earners and mothers.

★ Point out that loving others means giving of oneself and of one's time, energy, and/or money to others. This sharing of love does not necessitate reciprocation. Example: Sibling #1 helps sibling #2 with his homework. This doesn't mean that sibling #2 will let #1 ride his bicycle. One gives with the hope of being appreciated, but it is important to learn that love is offered for its own sake rather than in the expectation of love returned. Response to love can be negative or positive. The positive response can be offered in various ways. Perhaps the clearest and deepest are the words "I love you," but no less real is a warm embrace, a kiss, or the sharing of possessions.

★ Plan a meal to which each family member invites a friend

toward whom he or she has strong feelings (love). Ideally, each member of the family should invite people not related to one another. Example: Each of you has a friend in the Smith family. If you invite the Smiths as a family, you will be limiting the experience. Invite co-workers, schoolmates, neighbors, church friends. Share tasks in planning, preparing, and cleaning up.

★ Talk about problems of world starvation, if appropriate for the child with whom you are developing a relationship. Collect cans of soup and vegetables or money to donate to a charity. Involve a religious group, school class, or Scout group to help in this project, if appropriate. Pray together concerning the plight of others, and express your feeling of thankfulness for the benefits you and your child have.

★ Study and discuss your concern for ecology. Share your feelings concerning life, plants, and animals. You might begin by studying dinosaurs (most children love dinosaurs). Where were the dinosaurs? Where are their bodies now? Terms such as *extinction, endangered species,* and *depletion of resources* can be introduced. Visit a nature center or museum. Let your child suggest ways to show love for this earth.

★ Plant a garden in empty juice cans or in the yard. Share the care and maintenance of the plants with your child. Discuss the influence of sun and water on the growth of plants and vegetables.

★ Ask your child to draw posters or pictures concerning other living things. Does he or she understand what you are trying to teach? Does your child empathize with the plight of others? Can *you* empathize with the condition of others?

★ Talk about the people in helping professions. Do they have feelings for others? Examples: Does a medical doctor ever cry when someone is sick? Does a fireman ever feel frightened when he fights a fire? Is the child's teacher ever concerned about a child who has learning problems?

SUGGESTIONS FOR THE COGNITIVE DIMENSION

THE NATURE OF THE MIND

Current research on the brain is revealing information about the aggressive nature of learning. Children can process more information than was generally thought possible. Children's questions require that we listen and attempt to answer. Exchange dialogue with your child. Learn along with your child. Let your child know that you don't know everything. Show your child how to use a library to gain access to information.

★ Talk with children, but remember that knowledge is best understood when it is physically experienced. Example: The changing color of leaves in the autumn is better understood when you are in the woods gathering leaves. The use of books, pictures, or TV shows can help when a direct experience is impractical (riding the space shuttle to the moon; traveling by dog sled to the North Pole).

★ Remember that children learn differently at different ages. It would be useful to look through a child development book to learn specific skills associated with the age of the child with whom you are interacting. But a child's questions and responses will help to reveal his or her level of understanding.

★ Think together of ways human beings have changed the environment. Take a pretend trip through history: Put a blanket over a card table. Then pretend with your child that you are early man, shivering and cold in the wilderness; "discover" the blanket "cave" and the warmth cavemen must have felt. Watch a pretend thunderstorm when a flash of lightning strikes a tree, makes heat, and cooks a bird that had been in the branches. Try to imagine how cavemen learned to use fire, stone implements, and other tools.

★ By pretending, share the sense of accomplishment inherent in an appreciation of the human species, which survived and multiplied in warm and cold climates, as farmer and hunter, as nurturer and destroyer, as a creature living in a man-made city full of factories and traffic and as a modern-day pioneer, growing food organically and attaining self-sufficiency.

LEARNING AS A NATURAL OCCURRENCE

Learning does not require adult intervention. Children learn from other children and adults, from books and television. You, as a significant person in your child's life, will become one of your child's teachers in the process of nurturing.

★ Tell your child how well he or she learns, reads, or speaks. Give examples. A positive self-concept is a very important resource for each person in this contemporary society. The world will provide the "shock" factor—that a child is not the biggest, brightest, or best in intellectual or physical matters. It is the responsibility of adults—in this case, men—to act as reinforcers of the cognitive abilities that a child does possess.

★ Provide experiences that will allow your child to apply his or her knowledge to new situations. Examples: For a child who can identify the common barnyard animals, introduce pictures of birds, oxen, wolves, and other wild animals. Ask which barnyard animal this new creature is most like. If your child has musical interest, ask if he or she can play part of a scale by tapping glasses with a spoon. Then invite your child to experiment with a simple melody. If your preschooler has learned the consonant sounds, point to a familiar word. Ask your child to sound the consonants as you supply the vowel sounds. Enjoy discovering the word together. Once your child has mastered a 25-piece puzzle, make a more difficult puzzle available (as interest and finances warrant).

MEN AS TEACHERS AND LEARNERS

Think of yourself as a co-learner, sometimes with more experience than your child. Carry out activities in which your child is the "teacher." Listen as your child explains his or her understanding of a process. Example: how a nail holds pieces of wood together.

★ Be aware that your child may be surprised that he or she can teach you. Also, your child may be afraid to try a new skill for fear of being a failure in your eyes. It is important that your child understand that it is possible for all people to continue to learn if they are willing to seek new information. Your child also needs to know that learning is sometimes easy and sometimes hard. There are even times when we cannot gain a skill, no matter how hard we try, because we simply do not have the mental or physical ability.

★ Occasionally, tell your child something new you have learned that day, and ask if he or she has learned something new. *Listen* when your child explains a concept that is new to him or her.

★ Try some activities at which you both are very skillful, and others at which you both need to gain skill. Examples: mend a torn shirt, cook a meal, change the oil, wash the clothes. Show your child that you are willing to risk being less than perfect at a task.

★ Allow your child to learn and practice a skill until it becomes operational. For example, a mechanical skill such as hammering a nail is fully learned only after much practice. Be sure to say things such as, "I like the way you're holding the nail, so that your thumb is not near the head." Positive comments encourage your child to learn and not to feel ashamed or inferior.

★ Put the concept of competition into perspective. The American society is full of competition, from Little League and school grades to amount of money earned and social status. Does this emphasis help one become a fully functioning person? A focus on competition may prevent closeness between friends and block the communication of feelings. It may prevent one from trying a new activity or sport because of the discomfort of being a beginner.

LEARNING AT SCHOOL

Learning occurs both at school and away from school. However, much emphasis is rightly placed on academic skills. School is the child's work. Volunteer there if you can or *assist* in special projects, and attend school events. This shows your child that you are interested in his or her cognitive/academic development.

★ Visit the school when your child is in a play or project. Also visit during a normal school day. If possible, meet your child's friends and have lunch in the cafeteria.

★ Share your interests and skills with the class. This is generally appreciated by both teacher and students, especially since men assist in the classroom less often than women do.

★ Depending on your relationship to your child's family, it may be appropriate to attend parent-teacher conferences or become involved with disciplinary problems, sex education, or such matters. Even if you are not the biological parent or the guardian, this expression of interest may be welcome.

SUGGESTIONS FOR THE
PHYSICAL DIMENSION

BODY AWARENESS

An appreciation of the physical dimension of development can be nurtured early in a child's life. Children are usually quite active and often interested in demonstrating their capabilities. A sensitivity toward physical condition and ultimate performance helps a child define one ingredient of his or her selfhood. It is an area that needs emphasis, but it should not overshadow the other dimensions of growth.

★ Ask your child to think about his or her own physical appearance and note the similarities and differences as compared to other children (friends). Avoid judgments about differences or similarities. Point out that each person is unique in his or her physical development. Any differences noted do not carry "better than" or "not as good as" connotations. Help your child understand that phrases such as "bigger than" and "different from" do not mean that something is superior. Compare the sizes of some adults and the quality of those relationships.

★ As an entree into physical exercises, have the child experiment with you to see how much flexibility of movement he or she has. Begin by doing body twists, leg raises, deep-knee bends, and then sit-ups. (The child may have to approximate some exercises. Again, no judgment should be placed on what the child does—only an acknowledgment of the particular accomplishment. Let your child suggest some body movements—some silly body motions or dancing steps, Simon Says, Mother May I?—and follow his or her directions.

UNDERSTANDING BODY FUNCTIONS

A child's normal physical development is enhanced if he or she understands the way the body functions.

★ When you feel your child is capable, go to a library and locate a good set of encyclopedias. Look up material on anatomy or physiology. Show your child the muscular and skeletal connections in the body. Many encyclopedias have colored overlay charts which describe in detailed pictures the makeup and functions of the human body. Ask your child to draw a picture of his or her body as you do the same. Help your child learn to express him- or herself in art. Does the drawing reveal aspects of his or her self-concept?

★ Demonstrate for your child how various parts of the body are used to perform certain types of physical tasks. Example: As you lift something, both leg muscles and bicep muscles are necessary to perform the task. In this activity you can talk about the difference between physical strength and physical endurance. The idea of muscular power can also be demonstrated by noting that both a broad jump and a jump from a standing position require a quick release of physical force. In this way you can help your child understand the use of various parts of the body and the physical attributes that allow a person to accomplish certain activities.

★ Play a body-parts game. Place an object across the room. Ask your child to get it without using his or her feet or legs. Let your child place the object on a table; then *you* try to pick it up without using your hands. Walk without bending your knees. Each of you can think of other ways to demonstrate the usefulness of individual parts of the body.

★ To help your child begin to understand internal functions, observe a rag doll or a floppy stuffed animal. It has no skeleton and so cannot remain upright except when propped up. Use a nutcracker to demonstrate the work of teeth. A piece of celery in water colored with red food coloring will, after a while, illustrate the idea of blood moving throughout the body. Try to think of additional examples.

BUILDING APPRECIATION OF
PHYSICAL EXERCISE PLUS COORDINATION

Normal physical exercise can be fun in and of itself. Your child can participate in exercises that give him or her a sense of accomplishment in endurance and strength. It is important to help a child understand the relationship between physical fitness and health.

★ If you engage in exercise, allow your child to be an active participant. Simply walking around the block or down the street is a beginning. As you walk, ask what parts of the body are being exercised (feet, legs, arms, lungs, heart).

★ If you are involved in a physical-fitness program, allow your child to join you. This can be as elementary as basic calisthenics at home—knee bends, toe touching, leg raises, squats. For younger children, just modeling these exercises may be sufficient, whereas an older child can begin to do sets of exercises to build endurance and strength. Be aware that children's songs and games frequently include built-in exercise—"head and shoulders, knees and toes." School children usually have physical education programs and may bring home exercise ideas.

★ With a younger child, it is fun to roll a ball back and forth to develop physical coordination. A slightly older child can throw and catch a ball with the same purpose in mind.

★ Organize games and exercises that you and your child can play with family and/or friends. Frisbee games, ball games, and group exercises can be enjoyed while picnicking or cooking out.

★ Plan physical activities for the entire year. Brainstorm activities appropriate for indoor and outdoor settings for all seasons.

PERSONS WITH HANDICAPS

An awareness of the limitations of persons with physical handicaps is important. American schools, businesses, and industries are redesigning environments so that they are accessible to such people. Help your child to understand that persons with handicaps can be mobile in wheel chairs or specially designed cars, possess other developed skill areas, and have the same range of feelings as other people. Often a child will learn some of these positive concepts at school, where there may be a child with a handicap.

★ Talk to your child's teacher to learn how he or she is helping students develop a humanistic attitude toward persons with handicaps.

★ Discuss different types of disabilities. Point out how people can adapt to these conditions successfully. Focus on the support provided by wheel chairs, canes, and crutches.

★ Attend a local Special Olympics meet. Talk to the participants and show your child that you feel these children and adults are people who deserve respect and admiration.

★ Take out library books which describe conditions and true-life adjustments to such conditions.

★ Compare your own and your child's special abilities and lack of abilities to those of people with handicaps. Example: You have poor equilibrium and become dizzy while doing somersaults, but you can stretch beautifully.

SUGGESTIONS FOR THE SPIRITUAL DIMENSION

THE NATURE OF GOD

Spiritual development can be defined as an ever deepening relationship with God. This relationship grows by stages. To begin with, children learn to trust (or not to trust) those who love them. The nature of God begins as a general feeling of trust and awareness of caring. As children become very involved in their own physical selves, God takes on a physical form (like pictures they have seen, words they have heard, or a creation from their own imagination). Inquisitive elementary school children are intrigued by the miraculous power of God. They are beginning to relate to God as a Miracle Worker who can fulfill certain needs and desires. Only in later childhood is the relationship understood as that of a Spirit whose love always surrounds us and to whom we can respond with love and assurance.

★ Always speak of God with respect. All the time your child is developing a more mature concept of God, there should be that underlying feeling that God is special and important to you.

★ Ask your child who or what God is. By verbalizing, he or she may be able to think through his or her own ideas. Such a question will assure your child that you consider God to be a valid topic of conversation. Don't be "hooked" into giving a judgment about the child's ideas. A general but honest response could be something like, "We all have different ways of describing God, and that's all right. The most important thing to remember is that God loves you and each of us." Give your child security in God's love and concern for him or her.

★ Ask your child to tell you (or dictate while you write) some of the characteristics of one of his or her friends. Ask, "What is your friend Tom like?" You might also ask for a description of someone the child does not like. Then ask for some characteristics of God. Compare the verbal or written list of the friend with that of God.

★ Sing songs that tell about God. Your child's religious education teacher or take-home papers frequently have suggestions. Let the singing be spontaneous—as you take a walk, rake the leaves, take a trip. Don't belabor the point of a song by a lengthy explanation, but take time to talk if your child has a direct question, or seems puzzled, or if you have some personal experience you wish to share.

★ As you show affection to your child, occasionally mention that God loves him or her, also, and will never stop loving. As the occasion occurs, you can assure your child that though you may not like his or her behavior at times, your love does not change or stop—and that no matter what, God's love will never stop.

★ When you respond to a request to help the unfortunate, explain that because God loves you, you are able to love others. Point out times when your child has behaved in a loving way toward others. Older children can look in the newspaper for examples of persons who have behaved in loving ways (and in hateful ways).

CREATION

Even scientists who are unraveling the mysteries of the one-celled amoeba can be struck by the miracle of life itself and the infinite plan of our earth and the entire universe. You can help your child experience a sense of awe when observing his or her natural surroundings and the wonder of his or her own self. The next step is to couple this appreciation for all creation with a sense of gratitude and a feeling of responsibility for the care of ourselves and our world.

★ Take slow walks. Take turns pointing out pleasing scenes or objects. A simple statement that you are glad God planned for such a beautiful world is all that needs to be said.

★ As a real treat, stay up to watch the stars and the night sky. Somehow the concept of creation takes on a special meaning when we gaze out into the universe. An older child may be interested in identifying the various constellations. The library can help here.

★ Observe the weather. *Feel* the weather. Talk about the need for changes of season and different types of weather. When faced with some natural disaster caused by weather, your child can be helped to understand that weather gets out of control sometimes, just as we do. Think of examples when you or your child lost your temper, caught a virus, cut your arm. God planned for weather and for people; he allows them to run their natural courses.

★ Grow something, either plant or animal. This is a good way to appreciate one specific part of God's world and the wonder of growing things.

★ Conserve God's creation. Recycle metal, sand (glass bottles), and wood (newspapers). Put out campfires, plant grass or ground cover on banks to prevent erosion. Put on an extra sweater and turn down the thermostat a bit. God's world is for us to use, not to abuse.

MORALITY

Morality is fostered by learning to make ethical decisions. Children's understanding develops most clearly as they observe and experience moral teachings being lived out, so to speak, by those around them. If their parents, Big Brothers, peers, and the general public share themselves and their possessions, show respect for others and themselves, forgive one another, and respect life and the world around them, children will tend to absorb these qualities.

★ To be sure, there is a process children go through before they are established in the ability to make moral judgments. Young children "obey the rules" to avoid punishment. Younger elementary children who wish to excel will "do right" to be accepted and find a sense of satisfaction. Later they become concerned about approval by the group. Their moral decisions at this point are those that maintain compliance with authority and the law. It is not until some time in adolescence that youngsters are able to make moral decisions without regard to consequences (rewards, punishments, approval).

★ When your child seems to find it difficult to make moral choices in a certain area, try talking through a role-play situation. Example: If your child has been continuously taking items that belong to other family members, you might imagine with the child how he or she might feel if someone took one of his or her personal belongings. In this way, you place your child in the role of the other person and allow him or her an opportunity to struggle with moral choices. This kind of activity can also strengthen the capacity for empathy.

★ Make up little stories that describe situations where ethics are involved. Example: If a child sees another student cheating on a test, how should the child respond when he or she realizes the consequences for the other students? Take time to describe the situation and then talk about the possible choices. Don't hesitate to talk about some of the moral dilemmas at your place of work or in your personal life.
★ After reading stories or watching television programs, discuss situations in which people were taken advantage of. Think about ways in which their situations could have been improved.
★ Remember with your child how certain recent family conflicts were resolved. How were feelings handled? What was the extent of forgiveness among family members? Could there have been other outcomes? These kinds of questions can serve as the basis for future more positive types of family interaction.

PRAYER

Prayer begins as a routine shared by a child and another person. The language should reflect the child's general feeling of trust and confidence. It is normal for older children to begin to take the concept of God and prayer seriously when they are introduced to stories in the Bible, the Torah, or other religious books; they then begin to expect Omnipotent answers to requests. Eventually, prayer can be understood and practiced as a conversation between a human being and his or her Friend.
★ Bless the food at a meal. Let everyone have a turn. Intersperse rote blessings with more spontaneous prayers. Respect every idea sincerely expressed (perhaps, to the child, ketchup *is* the most important item on the table).
★ Teach a bedtime prayer that expresses confidence in God's care. Asking God to take care of us if we die during the night may not be the best way to teach trust, or the best way to put a child into a frame of mind for sleep.
★ Let your child hear you pray. Tell him or her, if you paused

to pray during the day. Let your child ask you questions about your prayer. Do not permit a judgment, just as you would not judge a sincere attempt on your child's part.

★ Introduce your child to children's books of prayers. When he or she is able to read, look at some of the prayers common to your own religious faith. Each of you could sit down with a paper and pencil and try writing a prayer to God in the same way you might write a letter.

RELIGIOUS TRADITION

Religious tradition includes the holy Book of a religious faith; holidays of special significance and the customs surrounding them; the act of worship; and the relationship of a person (and a family) to the whole community of believers. These form a framework in which a child can find his or her own sense of belonging. Many books, as well as religious education materials available at your place of worship suggest excellent ideas for carrying on religious traditions.

★ Read, tell, show pictures of, and sing about events in the holy Book. Help your child try to feel the emotions of the characters in the stories ånd relate those emotions to his or her own. Being able to recite a story means little unless a child is able to connect it to some personal experience or emotion. Share current stories in which the situations are similar.

★ Make some response to selected stories and encourage your child to do so. This might take the form of telling how the events in the story made you feel (joyful, angry, puzzled), talking about the point of the story, perhaps even discussing a personal act of kindness you might perform that would be in keeping with the lesson of the story. If you decide on some kind of project, be sure to carry it out.

★ Make a habit of carrying out certain religious rituals each year. Light the Hanukkah candles and say the prayer; light the Advent candles during the home ceremonies.

★ Prepare together in the kitchen for religious celebrations. Boil, dye, and decorate eggs for Easter as a symbol of new life; prepare the Seder Plate in observance of the flight from Egypt.

★ Sing hymns and other religiously oriented songs whenever the Spirit moves you or your child. An awareness of God's presence and love can be quite spontaneous, and music is a natural form of expression. These songs also help acquaint the child with part of the formal worship ritual.

★ Visit your place of worship at a time when services are not being held to allow your child to become accustomed to the room, the symbols, the prayer book, and other items. Help your child feel at home in this place of worship.

★ Attend worship services as a family. Even a young child can stand up or sit down with the group, turn the pages of the hymnal, listen to special music. Depending upon your child's age and the type of service, attendance for the entire time may not be warranted, however.

★ Introduce your child to some of your friends in the worshiping community and make it a point to meet some of his or her friends. Gather with others for times of fellowship as well as for worship. Make all these times special by your positive attitude.

APPENDIXES

ADULT'S INTEREST SURVEY

1. This is how I spend my time now.

   Activity   *Approximate Number of Hours Per Week*

   1.
   2.
   3.
   4.
   5.
   6.
   7.
   8.
   9.
   10.

2. These are the hobbies or interests I think I could share with my child(ren).

   Hobby or Interest   *Name & Age of Child(ren)*

   a.
   b.
   c.
   d.

3. I spend about this much time with my child(ren) now (hours per week).

   2   4   6   8   10   12

4. I would like to spend this much undivided time with my child(ren).

   2   4   6   8   10   12

5. These are the times when it would be most convenient for me to be with my child(ren). (Place a √ beside the possible choices).

_____ weekday evenings right after work
_____ weekday evenings after supper
_____ weekday mornings before work
_____ Saturday mornings
_____ Saturday afternoons
_____ Sunday mornings
_____ Sunday afternoons
_____ Sunday evenings

6. These are the times when I know my child does not have another activity scheduled. (Place an x beside the appropriate times on number 5. If you have more than one child, answer this question for each child.)

CHILD'S INTEREST SURVEY

Child's Name _____ Age _____

(If you have more than one child, complete a separate survey for each child.)

1. My child enjoys

_____ indoor activities
_____ outdoor activities
_____ both

2. My child enjoys

_____ quiet activities
_____ physical activities
_____ both

3. My child usually

_____ plays alone
_____ plays with a group
_____ some of both

4. What particular activities do you know your child enjoys?

a. _____
b. _____
c. _____
d. _____
e. _____

PROCESSING SHEETS

SHEET 1

(To be completed after sharing 12 to 16 activities.)

1. What have you discovered about yourself in completing these activities? What have you discovered about your child(ren)?

> *Self*   *Child(ren)*

2. Look at the Evaluation section of the activities you have completed. What seem to be strong areas in your relationship?

3. What areas to you think you need to improve? How would you like your child(ren) to improve?

> *Self*   *Child(ren)*

4. Other comments.

SHEET 2

(To be completed after sharing 24 to 32 activities.)

1. How is the use of these activities affecting your relationship with your child(ren)?

2. Compare your evaluation comments for the first 8 to 10 activities with your comments for the next 8 to 10 activities. Are there any differences? If so, what are they?

3. What areas do you think you need to improve? How would you like your child(ren) to improve? Are the areas needing improvement on Processing Sheet 1 similar to those on this sheet?

   Self   *Child(ren)*

4. Other comments.

SHEET 3

(To be completed after sharing 33 to 45 activities.
Complete a separate sheet for each child.)

1. Describe the relationship between yourself and your child in each of these areas.

   Social:
   Emotional:
   Cognitive:
   Physical:
   Spiritual:

2. Check one:
   _____ I am an effective model in this child's life.
   _____ I am not an effective model in this child's life.

   Why is this true?

3. What overall effects have these activities had on your family?

4. I have learned the following about myself and my child.

   Self   *Child*

5. What other steps do you plan to further improve your relationship with your child?

6. Other comments.

USE OF THIS BOOK
BY PROFESSIONALS

Although we have written directly to men, mothers and others will also find this volume useful. Professional educators, social workers, day-care workers, parent trainers, and family life educators (to name a few) could refer certain portions of the book to parents, who might be more willing to read several pages about child development than wade through an entire book. The opening remarks also create a sense of awareness of fathering and nurturing, to stimulate thinking about ways to establish positive adult-child relationships.

The activity section can be used to help families examine the quality of their relationships and to develop a more positive awareness of each member's place in the family group.

Some of the activities could be used as exercises in counseling sessions. People who work with groups of children might find ideas for occasional one-on-one sessions. Community education organizations that deal with parenting skills might also find this material pertinent.